OF
SATANIC
RITUAL
ABUSE

Equipping and Releasing
God's People For
Spirit-Empowered Ministry

Patricia Baird Clark

Restoring Survivors of Satanic Ritual Abuse
by: Patricia Baird Clark

The King James Bible was used for scripture references.

Interior Design and Cover: Leo Ward

PUBLISHED BY:
Five Stones Publishing
A DIVISION OF:
The International Localization Network
randy2905@gmail.com
ILNcenter.com

DEDICATION

This book is dedicated to...

God the Father who called me,
Jesus Christ His Son who empowers me,
And the Holy Spirit who directs me.

It is my prayer that this book will inform and encourage the Church to take her rightful place in ministering to God's most wounded lambs...the satanically ritually abused.

So glad God brought us together.
I look forward to our new friendship.

Patricia

TABLE OF CONTENTS

INTRODUCTION

There is a kind of abuse running rampant in America that the average person knows nothing about. It's the sort of thing we might believe happens in some foreign country but not here in America. However, it is going on here, and the church needs to know about it because the victims of this abuse (we call them survivors) are all around us, even in our churches, and they desperately need our help.

The existence of satanic ritual abuse and its accompanying devastation in the lives of myriad persons has long been hidden from our society. Even mental health professionals and the church have been unaware of its existence. It has become my commitment, through years of struggling for an understanding of this enigma, to expose this heinous perpetration. Through God's calling and preparation for ministry to satanically ritually abused persons, I have come to learn and understand much of this mystery.

Many people have never heard of satanic ritual abuse (SRA). Some of those who have heard of it doubt that it actually exists. There have been articles in secular and Christian periodicals and books claiming this kind of abuse is the figment of an overactive imagination...that persons who believe this kind of abuse occurs are excessively afraid of the Devil and see demons behind every bush.

There have been accusations made that false memories of abuse have been planted in a client's mind by the therapist—perhaps planted there while the client was under hypnosis. The fact that this has undoubtedly happened does not invalidate the truth that legitimate memories of severe abuse do sometimes surface many years after the occurrence of the abuse.

Amidst all the controversy are the severely satanically ritually abused persons who desperately need help. Unfortunately there are relatively few counselors who recognize this abuse or know how to deal with it once it is revealed. However, this picture is changing gradually. This is not to criticize the mental health profession. The fact is no university education can possibly prepare anyone to deal with SRA because SRA is a spiritual issue. The damage is done in the name of Satan and can only be undone by the power, love and wisdom of Jesus Christ.

I am concerned that counselors and pastors frequently are not trained to recognize SRA because Bible colleges, seminaries, and universities don't offer courses on this subject. It is an amazing fact that many persons who have experienced SRA have absolutely no memory of it and therefore have no knowledge of the root issue underlying their problems. Pastors seeing these symptoms in someone will often send them to a professional counselor. The professional counselor is trained to counsel according to counseling techniques rather than prayer and total reliance on the Holy Spirit. Few know how common SRA is or recognize its identifying characteristics. It is my prayer that this book will inform persons so that those suffering from this abuse will be identified and helped.

I am convinced that the ministry to these abused persons belongs to the church...not just to pastors but to certain laypersons called by God to come alongside and, with the help of the Holy Spirit, minister wholeness to these people. I don't want to call them counselors... counselors are people with psychology degrees, counseling techniques and malpractice insurance. I prefer to call these laypersons by some other term such as spiritual director, spiritual helper, spiritual friend, or minister. It is my belief that the spiritual nature of SRA requires spiritual ministry and anyone called by God who relies on the Holy Spirit can minister successfully to even the most severely abused. When it comes to SRA, the call of God is more important than counseling credentials.

This book exposes the purpose behind satanic ritual abuse, the psychological techniques used in this abuse, and how to undo, through the power of the Holy Spirit, the results of such abuse. Even though this sounds very dark and ugly, the glory and beauty of the Lord Jesus Christ are also revealed in the pages of this book. It is impossible to face triumphantly the heartbreak of SRA without the glorious presence of Jesus. It is also impossible to minister successfully in this arena without growing spiritually and coming to know Jesus Christ in a whole new dimension.

It is my hope that this book will help to dispel the belief held by many that SRA does not exist because dissociated memories are not reliable. Any spiritual director who relies totally on the Holy Spirit will find that dissociated memories are only a part of the SRA ministry. There are elaborate programming schemes found in many SRA persons that reveal definite evil genius and design. Demons manifest and say and do things that validate memories. Also we find analogous structures and programs in people who don't even know each other, that greatly validate the case for legitimacy of memories.

I vacillated between using the term MPD (multiple personality disorders) and DID (dissociative identity disorders) knowing that the counseling community uses DID but that church laypersons may be more familiar with MPD. However, more and more church people are becoming familiar with the term DID so I decided to stay with that designation.

Pronouns used will be in the feminine gender for the most part to avoid the clumsiness of writing his/her or him/her each time a pronoun is required. Even though men have been abused also, the majority of those seeking counsel for abuse issues are overwhelmingly women.

A few details have been changed to protect the identity and privacy of some persons whose experiences are mentioned in the book. The changes are slight and in no way change the veracity of the experience or the concept being explained.

This book would not have been possible without the help of several persons. I want to thank, first, my husband for his willingness to allow me to spend so much time in this ministry. He has had to do some things alone that we were used to doing together, and he has been willing to share our home with others so they could receive more concentrated ministry. It has been an adjustment for both of us. I thank him, too, for being a strong spiritual covering for me, for his help in editing the book and for his computer expertise.

I also want to thank Roger D. Osborn for his encouragement to begin writing the book. As the book progressed, there were times when I felt I couldn't do it, but he was a constant encourager. Roger, having 35 years experience in mental health administration and clinical practice with a Ph.D. in Health Services Administration, was able to read the book through the eyes of a medical and mental health professional thereby providing a balance to my totally biblical perspective.

And lastly I thank all the SRA persons who sat under my ministry; without them, there would be no book. In the beginning I made many mistakes for which I apologize. I felt as though I were in a flimsy rowboat in uncharted waters with sharks swimming all around me who had bitten off the oars. There was, however, a golden cord tied to the front of that little boat pulling me across the uncharted waters...the Holy Spirit was there guiding me. Hopefully, because of this book, others won't feel as lost as they minister to the survivors of satanic ritual abuse.

CHAPTER ONE

THE NEED FOR SPIRITUAL MINISTRY

There is a trend towards Satanism and witchcraft sweeping over America at this present time of such magnitude it is sucking in millions of people of all age groups. Little children cast spells on one another on their school playgrounds as they imitate their favorite TV super heroes. Harry Potter and his witchcraft and wizardry are being exalted in school classrooms all over this nation as teachers proclaim him to be a good role model for students. School libraries are filling with books on witchcraft, voodoo, and Satanism in all its forms. Psychic hotlines are flashed on our television screens and talk show hosts are featuring séances and encouraging their viewers to join them in contacting their deceased loved ones. Movies about Satan, witchcraft, and the evil supernatural are a delight to millions of moviegoers as Hollywood rakes in revenues in the billions.

Halloween is beginning to rival Christmas in popularity. When I was a child, Halloween was only celebrated for one day, but now almost the whole month of October is devoted to it. People are decorating their yards and houses much the same way as for Christmas with orange lights strung across the outline of their houses and evergreen trees covered with orange lights like Christmas trees. In stores, restaurants and offices employees dress in Halloween costumes, and decorations celebrating death and evil are everywhere.

America, once considered by many to be a predominantly Christian nation founded upon biblical principles, has become a bastion of paganism and evil. People wait in line for days or even weeks to buy tickets to a satanic rock concert while many churches have closed their doors for lack of parishioners. The church, called to be salt and light, has compromised with the world and succumbed to apathy, while prosperity rules.

Many have left the church or refuse to enter the church because of the obvious hypocrisy and lukewarmness displayed by many of its members. I believe many more will leave as the outpouring of demons into the people of this nation results in the unavoidable...persecution of the church. The Devil hates God and His people and when Satan gets an upper hand in a populous, persecution of the faithful is always the result. However, this will only play into God's plan and purpose serving to cleanse His church. When the church is cleansed, God will pour in His power and His supernatural. Underneath the surface of what appears to be a weak, sin-laden church is a sleeping giant beginning to awaken. When it does, the world will see the glory and magnificence of Christ Himself displayed in His people.

When those who have been deceived into following the Devil through occult practices begin to awaken to the fact that they are hopelessly enmeshed in a web of oppression and bondage, many will look to the church for help. We must be prepared. We must be emptied of self and filled with the Holy Spirit to the point others can sense the presence of God about us. It is the power of His presence that will break the bondage and deception of sin and heal broken hearts.

In Deuteronomy 18: 9 - 12 we read, *When thou art come into the land which the LORD thy God giveth thee, thou shalt not learn to do after the abominations of those nations. There shall not be found among you any one that maketh his son*

*or his daughter to pass through the fire, or that useth divina-
tion, or an observer of times, or an enchanter, or a witch, or a
charmer, or a consulter with familiar spirits, or a wizard, or a
necromancer. For all that do these things are an abomination
unto the LORD: and because of these abominations the LORD
thy God doth drive them out from before thee.*

The average person has no idea that children are being
made to pass through the fire in America today, but I submit
to you that it happens a lot. Many satanically ritually abused
(SRA) individuals have had memories of being forced as young
girls to have babies which were either burned alive or killed
and then burned. The SRA person who has received the satanic powers instilled in them through rituals will have been
given the power to walk on hot coals without being burned.
This is commonly done at rituals to demonstrate the powers
of the "chosen child." When these powers are displayed many
will pay money to the child's owners to have the privilege of
raping her to gain her powers for themselves. (See Chapter 5,
The Purpose of Satanic Ritual Abuse) This is ugly stuff but
this is what Satanism is all about. We need to get our heads
up out of the sand and be willing to accept the fact that this is
happening right now, here in America.

This is being done in secret but we need to take notice of
what is being done blatantly and openly in our society. That
which was once frowned upon and done in secret is being
brought out into the open and exalted. Fortune telling, haunt-
ed houses, horoscopes, contacting the dead, reading tarot
cards, and casting spells are becoming fashionable and acceptable in our society. People are no longer shocked by what
they see and hear. Some reality television programs are showing openly things that were once done secretly within satanic
rituals—things like insects crawling all over a person, walking
on hot coals, etc.

A friend of mine works in the library of a large public school in our city. Books on voodoo, cannibalism, satanic rituals and a handbook on forming a witches' coven complete with tax exempt status are some of the latest volumes on their shelves waiting to be read by young impressionable teens.

The Bible tells us that people who do these things are an abomination to God. According to Webster an abomination is something nasty, hateful, vile, loathsome and disgusting. This is what God thinks of these activities and yet our tax dollars are used to buy these books for our children and no one is complaining--at least not in this particular school.

Why did God forbid these activities? He gave us these laws for our own protection in much the same way that he gave instructions concerning cleanliness. God's people were instructed to wash after touching a dead body or a diseased person. God didn't tell them about microorganisms being the cause of disease. He simply said, Obey My commandments. They were to accept His laws and obey them believing that He was a good God who was instructing them out of the motive of pure love for their own well being.

We would do well to accept His laws regarding spiritual taboos with the same faith. God didn't forbid these activities to spoil our fun. He knew that when we participate in such practices, demons attach to us in much the same way microorganisms do when we handle contaminated things. These demons will deceive us and do us great harm.

We are forbidden to participate in occult activities not only because of the attachment of demons but also because these practices begin to remove the veil that God placed between us and the spiritual realm. Our heavenly Father purposely made us so that we cannot see or hear spirits. This is for our own protection. God knew that if we began to seek the supernatural to foretell the future or contact the dead we would be deceived. To begin with, only God knows the future. Fortune-

14

tellers get their information from demons, not God. They may believe they are getting it from God but they are deceived. They are right part of the time but they are often wrong and there is a heavy price to pay for seeking these things--demonic oppression.

Contacting the dead is impossible. According to the Bible when people die they either go to heaven or hell. They don't hang around interacting with human beings on earth. People who attend séances to contact spirits will meet spirits but they will not be those of departed human beings. They will be demon spirits impersonating the departed person. People who are deep into the occult will have spirits appear to them claiming to be famous persons or a deceased loved one. These are actually demons. Demons can appear in any form they choose. They will look and sound exactly like the departed human they are impersonating.

I do believe that angels can manifest to human beings and have heard some amazing stories of people being miraculously helped by these heavenly beings; however, we are not to seek them. Should we start seeking beings from the spiritual realm we will find ourselves being deceived by demons. We are to seek the Lord Jesus Christ and He will determine whether or not we need an angelic visitation.

I believe there will come a time when God will remove the veil and allow us to see into the heavenly realms that are presently invisible to us, but this will not take place until the coming of the Lord.

The New Testament points to this veil being removed when Jesus speaks prophetically concerning Nathanael in *John 1:47b...Behold an Israelite indeed, in whom is no guile!* And then says to him, *Verily, verily, I say unto you, Hereafter ye shall see heaven open, and the angels of God ascending and descending upon the Son of man.* To me this is saying there will come a time when we will have an open heaven but not until such time as there is no guile in us. To see into an open heaven is to see into the realm of the spirit where there are angels and God Himself. However, in addition to seeing into that glorious heavenly realm there is another supernatural realm of evil where Satan and his demons dwell. If we have the ability to see into the good supernatural we will also, unfortunately, see into the evil realm. Until we are perfected that is to remain closed to us for our own protection because, as the Bible warns us, Satan can appear as an angel of light. In our humanness we would be deceived.

The great 19th century Christian writer Andrew Jukes states in his book, *The New Man and the Eternal Life*:

> ...man is a spirit, in a house of clay, and therefore, though he knows it not, is an inhabitant of an inward, as well as of an outward, world. Outwardly indeed, as in the present body and its life, we are in a world lighted only by the sun of nature, but inwardly our spirits even now are in a spirit world, which only is not opened to the natural man, because to open it to such would be to open the dark world, into which by sin we all have fallen. (Jukes 1891, 14)

We who are Christians need to familiarize ourselves again with what God's word says about occult activities. If God says that wizardry and witchcraft are an abomination to Him, why do we have Christian leaders lauding and approving of the Harry Potter books? Why would we lift up as a hero and role model a child who practices such things? It doesn't take a lot of intelligence to see that our children will desire to do the same things Harry Potter is doing. Even little children have that "God shaped void" that needs to be filled. Children are longing for the supernatural powers they see in cartoon characters and children's stories on television and in movies.

Some Christian leaders have acclaimed Harry Potter because they see truth in some of the things he says. Are we blind to the fact that Satan always puts a little truth in with his deceptions? If he didn't, they wouldn't be so deceptive. Evil often comes to us disguised under a cloak of good. That's why we need discernment.

I speak from personal experience.

Thirty years ago, as a young adult, I was hungering for the supernatural. At the age of six I had asked Jesus to be my Savior, but I had never pursued a relationship with Him. My family attended church, but I thought it was boring. There had been times that I had attempted to read the Bible; however, it didn't seem to make much sense to me...but I was hungry for something. I now know that I was hungry for God, but I chose to seek Him in the wrong places.

In my craving for something more, I began reading books by the occult writers (whom I thought were Christians) Edgar Casey and Jean Dixon. I was fascinated by the supernatural and wanted to experience more in that realm. About this time my husband had finished his first year of seminary, and we moved to another state where he continued in another seminary while serving a small church of about seventy people.

In this small church were two women, identical twins, who befriended us and began to share with us about the supernatural giftings "God" had given them. They both could see and hear spirits, reveal a person's past, foretell the future and astral project. Their brother had been in Vietnam, and during that time they had visited him by means of astral projection. My husband had returned from Vietnam the year prior to his beginning seminary. Our time apart had been extremely lonely. The idea of being able to travel in the spirit fascinated me. How wonderful it would have been if we could have visited with each other while he had been away in the war! I desired these powers. I found myself wanting to be with these women as much as possible. All my spare time was spent reading books about the supernatural.

I am so thankful that my husband did not share my interest. One might question why he didn't warn me of the danger inherent in these activities. If one knew what was being taught in the seminary, one would no longer wonder. This liberal seminary actually invited a parapsychologist in to lecture the students on the merits of telepathy, extrasensory perception and clairvoyance. I went to school with my husband that day and sat in on the lecture!

One evening the twins invited us to one of their homes for dinner, and one of them offered to tell my fortune. She took a deck of cards and began laying them out on the table as she told my future. I asked her why she used the cards, and she explained that they provided something on which to concentrate while she listened to the spirits. The spirits were telling her my future. She claimed the spirit of my grandmother was around me. (I have never met this grandmother as she died before I was born, but I love her just from what my mother has told me about her. I've seen pictures of her, and she looked much like me. Of course, this was not my grandmother; it was a demon impersonating her. My fortuneteller was deceived even as I was.)

Much of what she said to me I no longer remember, except for one thing. She said that my husband and I, who have two daughters, would have a son. Both of the twins said they could see this son, and that when they both see something it always happens. I was thrilled. Of course we wanted a son.

Can the reader understand how good all of this seemed to one who was ignorant of the warnings against such things in God's Word? These women were in the church. They said that they got their information from God who had given them these wonderful gifts. They used their gifts to help others. I was totally deceived.

I thank God that this deception lasted only a few months. In my hunger to know more, I eventually found myself reading a book written by a Christian minister, Don Basham, entitled *Can A Christian Have a Demon?* In this book he quoted scriptures and explained why all the occult activities with which I had been so enamored were an abomination to God.

After reading this book, I prayed and asked God's forgiveness for seeking these experiences. I gathered up all the books and notes I had on the subject and took them to the burn barrel in the backyard. As I leaned over the barrel watching the books and papers curl up and turn black in the fire, a large horsefly landed on my leg and bit me. I remember thinking about the scripture that says another name for Satan is Beelzebub, lord of the flies. I laughed thinking how angry the Devil must have been at me now that I was free from his deceptions. Little did I know that the Devil doesn't give up that easily.

That night I went to bed early while my husband stayed up studying. I was in that "twilight zone" between sleep and waking when I saw them. There beside my bed hovering over me were two hideous black demons. I screamed out in terror. Their presence brought a horror over me that was indescribable. This type of experience was to haunt me nightly for the next six months. Many of these occurrences happened while I was sleeping. My husband would tell me the next day about how I sat up in bed screaming during the night.

I didn't realize that I needed deliverance. I had asked God's forgiveness and renounced the activities in which I had participated, but I had picked up some demons that were terrorizing me. As soon as I stopped pursuing the occult supernatural, I began to pursue Jesus Christ with even more fervor. I devoured the Bible. No longer did I have time for hobbies and meaningless pastimes. All my spare time was spent reading and memorizing Scripture. I had asked God to fill me with more of His Spirit and He had done so. No longer were the

Scriptures boring or beyond my understanding. Now the Holy Spirit was instructing me, and His Word had come alive.

As I continued to seek the Lord, He again closed over that veil that had opened the spirit realm to me because of occult activities. At the end of that six month period, the nightly demonic visitations ended, and I never again saw another demon nor had any fear of them; however, the effects of the soothsaying were not yet over.

In the back of my mind I couldn't stop thinking about that son the twins had "seen." Knowing that their information came from the wrong source didn't necessarily mean it was untrue, I reasoned. Sometimes fortune telling is accurate. What if this were God's plan? When I had burned all the occult books, I had also given away all our baby furniture, baby clothes and maternity clothes. I wanted to make it perfectly clear to God and the spirit realm that I wasn't putting stock in what those women said, and I was going to fully obey God, but the thought was there in my mind and wouldn't leave.

Five years later we moved to a new church and parsonage. This parsonage had a small room just off the master bedroom that would make a perfect nursery. The feeling that we should have that son wouldn't leave me, and I convinced my husband we should try. I did conceive a child and then lost it only a few days into the pregnancy. I don't understand all this but one thing I do know, I was set free from that thought which had been planted in me by those women. Five years after the encounter with the twins I was finally completely free.

I tell this story to illustrate the fact that whenever we participate in occult activities we enter into demonic bondage. I read a few books and had my fortune told one time and had this much trouble coming out. Think of all the bondage to be reaped by those who are more actively involved over a period of years; however, we need to understand that severe bondage can come upon persons for an entire lifetime from just one occult encounter. My bondage wasn't severe because I began to seek God with extraordinary fervor and I already had considerable stability in my life from having grown up in a loving Christian family. People from highly dysfunctional families, a description of multitudes of Americans today, will have far deeper bondage and greater difficulty finding deliverance.

Troubled Youth

If there are any doubts about the emotional problems millions of American children are experiencing, the *Time Magazine* cover article of August 19, 2002 entitled "The Young and Bipolar" should dispel them. Beneath the cover picture of a nine year old child who suffers with this disorder is the question, "Why are so many kids being diagnosed with the disorder once known as manic depression?"

The article inside explains that this disorder is showing up in children at an alarming rate, and mental health experts have no explanation for why this is happening. The average age for the onset of the illness used to be the early 30s but has fallen in a single generation to the late teens. Experts estimate that an additional one million preteens and children may be suffering from the early stages of bipolar disorder.

No one knows why all these children and teens are sick. Some scientists wonder if there is something in our environment or modern lifestyle that is affecting them. Others believe something is wrong with their genes.

There is a listing of forty symptoms of bipolar behavior including the following:

has seen or heard hallucinations; is fascinated with blood and gore; has made clear threats of suicide; curses viciously in anger; has protracted, explosive temper tantrums or rages; lies to avoid consequences

21

of actions; blames others for his or her mistakes; has destroyed property intentionally; exhibits inappropriate sexual behavior; is willful and refuses to be subordinated; has night terrors or frequently wakes in the middle of the night; sleeps fitfully or has difficulty getting to sleep; exhibits excessive anxiety or worry.

I am sure by now many of my readers know where I am going with this. We can approach life from the standpoint that there is no God, everything has a scientific explanation and the Bible is an ancient book with interesting stories that are probably mostly myths. If this is our concept of reality, we can read this *Time* article and wonder why this enigmatic epidemic that is destroying the lives of our youth has happened.

Conversely, we can believe in the God of the Bible—a loving heavenly Father who knows us and loves us perfectly and has given us the Bible as a roadmap for life. With this approach to life, we can see into our society with spiritual eyes and look beneath the surface and see the societal consequences for having rejected God and ignored His loving principles for successful living.

Because I have ministered to satanically ritually abused people for many years, I have seen the manifestation of countless demons. As these demons manifested, I witnessed distinct changes in the behavior of the people to whom I was ministering. I have become very familiar with the way demons make people act, and I see no difference between their behaviors and the behaviors listed for a disease known as "bipolar." I'm not saying there is no such thing as bipolar disease or that something could not be physiologically wrong with a person's brain causing them to exhibit these behaviors. However, I think we need to be open to the possibility that young minds filled with scenes from satanic television shows and movies and stories of sorcerers and witches, might, just might, be troubled by demonic oppression.

One illustration comes to mind. I ministered to a satanically ritually abused woman who was unable to drive. I would pick her up and take her to church. For a period of several months while she was experiencing her most severe memories, she would try to open the door and jump out while I was driving. We have automatic door locks on our car, and I would drive with my left hand depressing the lock so she couldn't get out. Demons would be speaking out of her, and I would bind them until we got to church where I would cast them out in my office before the church service began. There were times when I had her in my office for ministry during the church service, and she would threaten to tear off her clothes and run through the church stark naked in order to disrupt the service. This was, of course, a demon that I cast out, and then she was perfectly normal and able to return to hear the rest of my husband's sermon.

With this in mind, read these first two sentences from the aforementioned *Time* article. (I have chosen to change the names of the persons named in the article.)

"It wasn't every day that Jane Smith raced down the streets of Miami at 70 m.p.h. But then it wasn't every day that her daughter Gracie hallucinated wildly, trying to jump out of the car, pulling off her clothes and ranting that people were following her..."

As I read this I thought, "This sounds familiar to me. I've been through this scene several times." At the hospital this girl was strapped to a gurney, administered sedatives and admitted to the hospital for two weeks. She was released with "a therapy plan and a cocktail of drugs."

If someone were to suggest that this girl might be exhibiting behavior caused by demon possession, they would probably be ridiculed and laughed out of the hospital. One wonders how many children and teens in America today are on prescription drugs simply because they have dabbled in witchcraft—whether it be Anime, Harry Potter, Dungeons and Dragons or school library books on witchcraft—and are suffering the consequences.

When we minister to troubled people we need to realize that underneath their severest problems may lurk demonic oppression. We'll deal with this more thoroughly in the chapter on demons, but it is important to know that demons may affect people's thinking to the extent they are incapable of receiving the truth until the demons are renounced and removed.

It is often advisable to inquire into the person's possible participation in occult activities. Most people when asked about such matters deny having any interaction with them. It's interesting that when specifically asked about each activity by name, almost everyone has participated to some extent. Today going to a movie can bring demonic oppression on someone. Movies designed to frighten their viewers can cause demons of fear to come upon those who watch them.

Some of the occult activities we should inquire about include: reading or telling horoscopes, hypnosis, casting spells, charming warts, hex signs, voodoo, martial arts, water witching, blood pacts, magic 8 ball, séances, automatic writing, astral projection, fortune telling, reading tea leaves, crystals, crystal ball, extrasensory perception, yoga, Ouija board, psychic healing, good luck charms, handwriting analysis, levitation, clairvoyance, drugs, Eastern mysticism, and religious cults. Any involvement in any of these activities needs to be repented of and renounced.

The Bible instructs us concerning witchcraft and occult practices in several places. A few of these may be seen below:

Galatians 5:19 - 21 *The acts of the sinful nature are obvious: sexual immorality, impurity and debauchery; idolatry and witchcraft; hatred, discord, jealousy, fits of rage, selfish ambition, dissensions, factions and envy; drunkenness, orgies, and the like. I warn you, as I did before, that those who live like this will not inherit the kingdom of God. (NIV)*

1 Samuel 15:23 *For rebellion is as the sin of witchcraft, and stubbornness is as iniquity and idolatry.*

2 Chronicles 33:6 (concerning wicked King Manasseh) *And he caused his children to pass through the fire in the valley of the son of Hinnom: also he observed times, and used enchantments, and used witchcraft, and dealt with a familiar spirit, and with wizards: he wrought much evil in the sight of the LORD, to provoke him to anger.*

The Bible makes it perfectly clear that witchcraft is sin and that to participate in such activities will provoke God to anger. (Please understand God is NOT angry with any SRA persons who were subjected to mind control and participated in occult activities as a result. I am thinking of our nation and our turning away from God to seek idols.)

A greater list of the evils that befall a society that turns away from God may be found in Deuteronomy 28. It is much too long to quote here, but they include starvation, confusion, pestilence, war, blight, mildew, severe weather, drought, boils, madness, blindness, incurable skin diseases, destruction of family, loss of property, locusts, worms, crickets, financial ruin, destruction of towns and cities, plagues, chronic sickness, death, a takeover by foreigners, etc. The list is long and many of these things are coming upon America today. It is far worse to have known God and then rejected Him than to have never known Him at all. May God have mercy on America, a nation who has known Him as none other, and now won't even allow Him into the schools. We are already seeing the results.

Human beings are religious by nature. If we turn away from the one true God we are going to worship something else whether we realize it or not--family, sex, drugs, material things—the list is endless.

We see in our nation today a tremendous hunger for the supernatural and for power. The Devil is making sure that we have full access to every mystical experience we could possibly want. I recently saw on television a news commentator interviewing a witch. She was surrounded with herbs and potions as she explained that people can have whatever they want through witchcraft. If you wanted a husband or wife, money, a good job, whatever--she had a potion that would do the job. She then recited a little six-word, rhyming spell for getting a parking spot. I saw this several months ago and still remember the rhyme. Millions of Americans saw that program. I wonder how many, when exasperated over the inability to find a parking space, may have uttered that little spell and gotten results. That one experience could bring many into the initial stages of occult entrapment.

When we minister to those who have been abused in satanic rituals, we will find that they have been forced to participate in many, if not all, of the occult practices we've mentioned. This is one reason they need to go through their memories-- they need to renounce these things and get free of the demons that are behind them. As we minister to these most severely wounded people, we must be able to bring the presence of Jesus to them. Only His presence can heal their deep wounds and mend their broken hearts.

CHAPTER TWO

THE GREAT EXCHANGE

I sense changes brewing in our land--changes that are going to affect our lives drastically in the not-too-distant future. We have been a prosperous nation because God has blessed us and because we have been a free people. The only way people can be free is if they are moral. In 1835 Alexis de Tocqueville wrote the following in his *Democracy in America*:

> I sought for the greatness and genius of America in her commodious harbors and her ample rivers—and it was not there...in her fertile fields and boundless forests and it was not there...in her rich mines and her vast world commerce—and it was not there. Not until I went into the churches of America and heard her pulpits flame with righteousness did I understand the secret of her genius and power. America is great because she is good, and if America ever ceases to be good, she will cease to be great. (de Tocqueville 1835)

Things are different in America today. Yes, there are some pulpits ablaze with righteousness but all too many offer a man-centered, watered-down, social gospel giving people license to do whatever they want. The church appears to have been more influenced by the world than the world has been by the church.

27

In *Think Like Jesus*, George Barna states, "Ninety-one percent of all born-again adults do not have a biblical worldview; 98 percent of all born-again teenagers do not have a biblical worldview." According to Barna, a biblical worldview includes the following beliefs:

- God is the all-knowing, all-powerful Creator of the universe who still rules that universe today.
- When Jesus Christ was on earth He lived a sinless life.
- Satan is not just a symbol of evil but is a real, living entity.
- A person cannot earn his or her eternal salvation by being good or doing good things for other people; that salvation is a free gift of God.
- Every person who believes in Jesus Christ has a personal responsibility to share his or her faith in Him with other people who believe differently.
- The Bible is totally accurate in all that it teaches. (Barna 2003, 22, 23)

What hope is there for our nation when even the church does not believe God's Word? How can we stand against the world's slide into the moral abyss of sin and Satanism when we have forsaken the biblical absolutes that give power and strength to the Christian life?

When moral restraints are cast aside, freedom is replaced with anarchy. Anyone who watches the evening news programs must see that anarchy is boiling just beneath the surface of our society. It erupts now and then in looting and mass shootings, but order is restored and life seemingly goes on as usual. Many of us sense that one of these days there is going to be some issue that will blow the lid off, and all hell will break loose. When it does, we can expect the freedom and prosperity we all love to be greatly diminished.

The dysfunction and disintegration of the family structure along with other factors have resulted in a large segment of our population having neither a healthy identity nor the ability to relate well with others. Many escape their inner pain through their addictions. Many of these addictions are maintainable because of the affluence of our society. Should we suddenly lose this availability of goods and services, many addictions will go unfulfilled resulting in a lot of desperate and even suicidal people. This will put a great strain on the mental health community. It may also cause a total disruption of our entire society.

When speaking of addictions we may think about drugs, alcohol, etc. but there are many other addictions that would suddenly go unfulfilled should a major disruption of power or a lapse in the flow of goods and services occur in our nation. What about the person addicted to electronics? Many people have not developed a life or identity apart from their TV's or computers. Others are able to cope only when they can go shopping. Others have to play the stock market or eat continually.

At some point soon I believe God will allow events to take place in the lives of millions of people that will cause them to have to come to grips with two major factors--identity and relationships. Many persons will find themselves being shaken to the very core of their being in the area of their own identity and also the corporate identity of our nation. When this happens, relationships will be crucial. We may suddenly find that we need each other, but that we've never learned to relate, trust or interact with one another. This could bring a season of great crisis.

I foresee a time in the near future when we will need to depend on God for things that we have taken for granted. We're going to have to rid ourselves of our old ways of thinking and doing and exchange them for God's ways. This is what I mean when I say the "great exchange." We are going to have to exchange our own natural strength and understanding for faith in God and His supernatural power for all things. This will apply not only to our daily lives but also to our ministry to others.

Relying on our own understanding or on mental health professionals may have brought results in the past, but we are entering into a time when I propose we will find these ways to be ineffective. Counseling techniques can't help people who are demon oppressed, demon possessed or under curses. Our natural understanding will not be effective in addressing the spiritual problems we will encounter. Increasingly people are going to mental health professionals with these kinds of problems and neither they nor the counselor recognize that the problem is spiritual.

Witchcraft is spreading like wildfire across America. Just a few hours ago I was talking with a friend who works in a school library. The head librarian had just told her she was going to take home a new book on witchcraft because she was hoping to put a spell on another librarian whom she considers to be her rival. This is a woman with a master of library science degree with a responsible position in the city school system saying she is going to cast a spell on another librarian! The librarian she wants to curse is the one who has been ordering the books on witchcraft in the first place!

Just as the essence of Christianity has served as a bulwark against the tides of evil in our nation, it has done the same in our schools. However, with the consistent and continual eradication of Christian foundations from our public school systems, the floodgates have been opened to new areas of evil. I have no doubt that this librarian can put a spell on the other woman. Both women are going to find their lives more chaotic than they are already. They are both going to need help somewhere down the line because they are dabbling in the evil supernatural where everybody eventually gets hurt.

I propose that not only do we need to exchange our old ways of doing things for God's ways, but also we need to exchange our very life for His. *Galatians 2:20: I am crucified with Christ: nevertheless I live; yet not I, but Christ liveth in me: and the life which I now live in the flesh I live by the faith of the Son of God, who loved me, and gave himself for me.* As we are willing to die to our own selfish ways, we will be filled with His life. The more we pour out our life to others, the more He pours His life into us until our life becomes His life. This is vitally important. This is the secret for success in our own life and in the lives of those seeking our help. Through this principle comes the power and love of His presence to "set the captives free."

Major Ian Thomas explains:

On the third morning after His crucifixion, the Lord Jesus Christ rose from the dead and appeared to His disciples. He instructed them for some forty days and then ascended to the Father. On the first day of Pentecost He returned, not this time to be with them externally—clothed with that sinless humanity that God had prepared for Him, being conceived of the Holy Spirit in the womb of Mary—but now to be in them, imparting to them His own divine nature, clothing Himself with their humanity, so that they each became "members in particular" of a new, corporate body through which Christ expressed Himself to the world of their day. He spoke with their lips. He worked with their hands. This was the miracle of new birth, and this remains the very heart of the Gospel!...The One who called you to minister to the needs of humanity is the One who by your consent ministers to the needs of humanity through you! (Thomas 1951, 14, 15)

When our spiritual directing is based upon the spiritual principle stated above, each session becomes an exciting adventure. We begin to realize that Jesus Christ is with us and in us, guiding us and giving us the power to accomplish the impossible. There is no problem too difficult for Him. He understands the root causes for the problems of those we are trying to help, and He will begin giving us discernment and wisdom to bring people out of their misery.

When we change over to total dependence on God and expect His supernatural help, we will find that troubled people will improve more quickly than with conventional methods. This will be an important factor if the numbers of those seeking help increase the way I am expecting. The following is an example of something being accomplished in one session through God's supernatural help that otherwise might have taken many weeks or months.

Every good minister knows that to be effective we must develop the trust of those to whom we minister. Sometimes this trust comes only after several meetings--especially when there has been severe abuse.

A thirty-five-year-old woman came to me for her first session. She had undergone counseling previously at a local mental health center and knew that she had been satanically ritually abused. This was her first time to come to a church for help and this may have contributed to her nervousness. We were also of different races, and she had experienced much persecution from members of my race. Trust may have taken considerable time to develop...but God had a plan.

We were sitting in our church that happened to be attached to the parsonage where my husband and I lived. As we talked, I began feeling a severe pain in my right side. I had never experienced such a pain. It soon became unbearable to the point that I was no longer able to continue. I informed her that I had a terrible pain on my right side and asked her to please go over to the house and ask my husband to help me. At her request he came over, and by then I couldn't move. I asked him to please pick me up in the position I was in and take me in the house and lay me on the bed, which he did. Fortunately I am a small woman and he is a strong man! As soon as he laid me on the bed the pain left.

Feeling very foolish I went back into the church where this lady had remained. As I told her about the pain in my right side leaving just as suddenly as it had come, she had a strange expression on her face. She said, "You're not going to believe this, but I have had a severe pain in my right side since I was twelve years old, and it just left!"

Needless to say, I had gained that woman's trust in one meeting, but it was the supernatural power of God that accomplished it. God knew that I was committed to Him and His purpose, and He had my permission to do anything He wanted with me.

There may come a time in our country when prescription drugs may not be as available or affordable as they are presently. There seems to be a trend in this direction as insurance premiums, co-payments and prices of medications go up while insurance coverage goes down. It has been my experience that prayer can accomplish as much or more than drugs in helping satanically ritually abused persons. Actually prayer is much better because there are no bad side effects and no insurance hassles with which to deal.

Every ministry session should begin with prayer to commit the entire time into God's hands. It is by prayer that God pushes up dissociated or repressed memories. In prayer all the lies of darkness are renounced, and the truth is confessed. Forgiveness is expressed through prayer. Breaking of curses and calling upon God's help for casting out demons is all a part of prayer. In prayer we ask God to minister His presence to the one we are helping. Actually prayer should be recognizing that Jesus is the third person in the room with the spiritual director and the survivor, and He should be included in all that is done.

Survivors of abuse should never try to experience their memories for therapeutic reasons when alone or attempt to cast out demons without the spiritual director present. To do so could cause problems. Memories are usually too painful to handle alone. It is the spiritual director who can bring comfort and the Lord's presence into the memory. He/she should be present to help deal with the demons because the wounded person alone could be overpowered by them.

Medications

There can be no doubt that psychotropic medications do have their place in helping emotionally disturbed people. I am not against medications; however, I prefer the people I am working with not take anything stronger than a mild antidepressant. With God's help we have been able to work through even the most severe episodes of trauma, panic attacks, depression, etc. The point I want to make is that often our first response is to seek the professionals and medication before we've given God a chance to move supernaturally in a situation. Experiencing the supernatural manifestation of God when one is enduring painful memories brings tremendous encouragement and hope, not only to that individual but also to the spiritual director.

Another thing that needs to be considered when dealing with SRA is that most of these people have been drugged by their perpetrators. Frequently this results in them having a fear of taking any kind of medicine. Several times I've had difficulty convincing them they need to take even a mild antidepressant. I try to let the Lord lead concerning this issue. He alone knows whether or not one can process memories without any medical help. One of the women I helped told me that the effect of taking some of the stronger psychotropic medications was to open her more to the spirit realm resulting in demonic visitations which only increased her distress.

Professional counselors working in conjunction with a psychiatrist have the option of recommending medications be given to an individual. I foresee a time when the numbers of persons needing ministry for emotional problems will far exceed the availability of professional counselors. It is my desire to see ministers and other concerned Christians who don't have counseling credentials involved in ministering to emotionally disturbed persons. Not all spiritual directors will have the option of consulting a medical professional. However, it has been my experience that if my survivor friend asked her family doctor for an antidepressant and explained she was going through ministry for childhood abuse, the doctor was willing to prescribe the medication.

According to Dr. Roger Osborn, an experienced mental health professional,

> Spiritual directors might wish to cultivate consultative relationships with Christian physicians who would be open to medication recommendations. This means that spiritual directors should become very knowledgeable about the various psychotropic medications, potential side effects, and potentiating effects. There might be a tendency for spiritual directors to turn to the so-called alternative medications. Not all are equally effective. Some can have harmful side effects, particularly if they are not carefully formulated. Some may not have the amount(s) of therapeutic content to which they purport. There can be potentiating effects of some of these alternative medications when taken in combination with certain prescribed medications. Some well-meaning Christian counselors also market vitamins

and minerals in conjunction with their practices. This, aside from being generally accepted as unethical, can be a dangerous practice because not all vitamins and mineral dosages are benign."

God purposely put me in situations of ministering to His most severely abused women with no one to call upon for help but Him. I had no support team or medical professional help of any kind. Many times I would have reached out for help had I known whom to call upon. We have moved often, and I have not known anyone in the medical field well enough to trust with the knowledge of what I was dealing with. Satanic ritual abuse is extremely controversial, and most medical professionals would assume that only the most educated mental health professionals would be qualified to work with these people. However, as we read in 1 Corinthians 1:27-29...*God has chosen the foolish things of the world to confound the wise; and God hath chosen the weak things of the world to confound the things which are mighty; and base things of the world, and things which are despised, hath God chosen, yea, and things which are not, to bring to nought things that are: that no flesh should glory in his presence.*

The Lord has called me to be a pioneer to forge a pathway out of the natural into the supernatural in the field of ministry to abused persons. As a pioneer I have had to work alone calling only upon the Lord for understanding and help. Believe me, if there had been any other way I would have taken it, but our Lord knows how to put us where He wants us in order to accomplish His purpose in us and through us. As a pioneer I have made many mistakes and learned most things the hard way. I have had to experiment to discern what works and what doesn't work.

Throughout this ministry I have learned that many physical problems arise with the ritually abused that may be healed through spiritual means. My first experience in this area was about twenty years ago. At that time it took me a month to deal with something that I would now be able to handle in a few minutes, but I was learning, and learning takes time.

During that first ministry encounter I learned about the correlation between drugs and the spirit realm. I'm not talking about pot, cocaine, LSD or heroine. I'm talking about something as simple and common as aspirin. The New Testament Greek word for "sorcery" is *pharmakeia*, from *pharmakeus*; which means "medication (pharmacy), i.e. (by extens.) magic (lit. or fig.):sorcery, witchcraft." Notice the words *pharmacy* and *medication* are associated with sorcery and witchcraft. Witchcraft always involves demons. It is demons that give witches their powers and go forth to administer their spells. Here we see a connection between drugs and demons.

Let me hasten to say that I find nothing wrong with taking medication when one is sick. Aspirin, antibiotics and many other drugs have been given to us by God to help us when we are attacked with sickness. The connection I was seeing between drugs and demons was a good connection as will be shown in the following account. This was an experience in which I learned that deliverance ministry can sometimes accomplish the same results as medicine.

When God was first introducing me to ministry for severely abused persons, a young woman suffering with severe emotional problems stayed in our home for about a month. Shortly after her arrival she began feeling like she had a fever. We checked her temperature and found it to be 100°. I started to get her an aspirin, but she said, "No, wait! Maybe it's a demon. Why don't you see if you can cast it out?"

I never would have thought of such a thing, but I agreed. Sternly I commanded the demon causing the fever to leave in the name of Jesus Christ. It readily came out with the manifestation of coughing. We checked her temperature again and it was normal. This was one of my first experiences with deliverance ministry, and I was thrilled over what had taken place. I began to envision myself going into hospitals and healing all the sick people. Little did I know...!

The next morning the fever returned, only this time it was higher--101°. I cast it out again. We checked her temperature and it was again normal. She seemed to be fine; however, the fever returned later that afternoon. This time I suggested she take a couple of aspirin, which she did. A little later her temperature registered normal. The fever would leave through deliverance or by use of aspirin.

The fever persisted over the next four weeks with ever increasing frequency and escalating temperatures. Sometimes I would cast it out and sometimes she would take aspirin or Tylenol. The results were the same. This fever was caused by a demon; therefore, we would have to deduce that a common drug found in almost every medicine cabinet in America can control, to some extent, a certain demon.

The last night of her month-long stay with us, I was up all night ministering to her as her temperature repeatedly soared to 106°. I had decided that this was her last night at our house, as I was afraid she would die. She had adamantly refused to see a doctor, but I knew when I was in over my head. I had done all I could do.

About six the next morning, she awoke from a dream and told me that God had revealed to her why the fever kept returning. Her mother was jealous of her being at my house (even though she was a married woman who had left home years ago). Her mother and her brother were sending a curse against her, and if we would break the curse, the fever would leave. We prayed to break the curse, and the 106° temperature left immediately and never returned.

(Please let the reader understand that not all fevers are demonic. A fever is usually the body's way of fighting off disease. This *particular* fever was a curse.)

This was my first experience with breaking curses. Since that time I probably have broken hundreds of them, as they are commonly sent against the satanically ritually abused. When SRA persons begin having memories and breaking free from their bondage, the cults and/or family members will repeatedly send curses against them that will manifest as physical afflictions. It can be a migraine headache, fever, excruciating stomach pains ... basically a person can feel anything that can be done to a voodoo doll and more. A voodoo doll can be held over a fire, poked with pins, cut with knives, impaled on a stick, or whatever else can be conjured up by a demon-filled mind. The SRA person has been programmed for a susceptibility to voodoo curses. They will need considerable help to overcome this tendency.

It is common in the mental health field to use drugs for calming hysterical or delirious persons. Many times in an abuse ministry situation, I have been faced with someone who was totally hysterical and out of control, but I had no access to drugs; however, I had access to Jesus Christ. I have been able to lay my hand upon their head and ask Jesus to let His power come over them. He has caused them to immediately "pass out" and go limp for a minute or two. When they come back to consciousness they are again in control. It is amazing.

When God calls a person to minister to the satanically ritually abused, He intends to fully equip them for successful ministry. This is one reason why it is important that only those persons who are called by God to this ministry be involved in it. Only God can release satanically ritually abused people from what the Devil has inflicted upon them through the cults. The spiritual director must approach each ministry session in faith believing that Jesus is there alongside to guide, protect and supernaturally administer whatever each situation requires.

Called to Ministry

Several years ago, a man in our church with a prophetic ministry began speaking to me about a ministry to which God was calling me. He said God was going to bring me His most severely troubled people, and I was going to bring them into wholeness. I found this word exciting and also frightening because I had absolutely no idea how to do it. What did I know about psychology? I felt totally inadequate for such a ministry.

His words proved to be true. It was not long after that that I became aware of satanic ritual abuse, and people with this problem began showing up at my doorstep asking for help. Their problems were gargantuan and I was continually faced with strange phenomena that totally baffled me. I didn't know what to do, but the amazing thing is, that is exactly what God wanted—someone who didn't know what to do! The most important thing was that I was called by Him to do it. The next lesson I learned was to let Him do it through me!

Facing enormous problems with no knowledge of what to do is a humbling experience. We don't like being in these kinds of situations, but they are good places to begin letting God be God. I was learning to depend on God rather than my own resources. He was teaching me humility, a lesson I am still learning. Andrew Murray explains:

> The creature has not only to look back to the origin and first beginning of existence, and acknowledge that it there owes everything to God; its chief care, its highest virtue, its only happiness, now and through all eternity, is to present itself an empty vessel, in which God can dwell and manifest His power and goodness.
>
> The life God bestows is imparted not once for all, but each moment continuously, by unceasing opera-

tion of His mighty power. Humility, the place of entire dependence on God, is, from the very nature of things, the first duty and the highest virtue of the creature, and the root of every virtue. (Murray, 11, 12)

When we face ministry situations with a total dependence on God, we become conduits through which His healing power and love can flow. Our first commitment needs to be to God Himself, a commitment that entails daily prayer, Bible reading, and Bible *study.* We need to be under authority in a good, Bible-believing church and have accountable relationships. If we don't have healthy relationships with other Christians— relationships in which we don't talk about abuse—we can be sucked into an unhealthy preoccupation with the subject of Satanism and abuse.

After years of helping SRA persons come out of their bondage, I have come to the conclusion that we don't have to be professional counselors to help even the most deeply troubled people. I have also come to believe that most of these people will not be set free from the effects of their abuse without some sort of relationship with their spiritual helper—the kind of relationship that would not be possible in a professional counselor/client setting. The most severely abused will need the most time and relationship. I took one woman through her memories in a year. We met once a week and rarely talked on the phone in between her weekly appointments. She was completely set free and went on to get married and live a normal life; but she was the exception. The duration and severity of her abuse was far less than anyone else's I have seen. All satanic ritual abuse is severe, but the duration and depths of abuse will vary. Another woman was totally shattered by her abuse. She needed daily attention and lived with us for months at a time. Without this kind of relationship she never would have been healed.

After coming to these conclusions on my own, I was totally thrilled to read what Larry Crabb was saying in his book, *The Safest Place on Earth:*

> Western culture has wrongly divided the territory into spiritual problems and psychological problems. We assign pastors and nice Christian people to deal with the first sort. They pray, discuss biblical passages, apply biblical principles, and nourish faith. Trained specialists are called in if the problem is thought to be psychological, something emotionally or relationally disturbed that prayer and biblical exhortation don't seem to touch. We think of these disturbances as diseases and disorders of the psyche that therapists must treat.
>
> But that's wrong. Psychological problems at root are spiritual problems. People suffering with them need spiritual counseling. (Certain symptoms may reveal a physical disorder, in which case neither therapist nor pastor can help. A physician is needed.) But spiritual counseling is too often thought of as superficial, structured discipleship: Memorize these verses, pray more, stop doing that, and don't miss church.
>
> In my view, spiritual counseling (or spiritual direction) does everything we now assume can only be done in psychotherapy. It probes the darkness of our deceived and defensive hearts...It looks for life that has survived terrible assaults...It enters the depths of pain and agony...And it provides an opportunity to relate in ways that heal...(Crabb 1999, 180)

Larry Crabb, the man saying we don't need the trained specialists, is a Ph.D., and has been a licensed psychotherapist for over thirty years. He is director of New Way Ministries and founder of the Institute for Biblical Community. I have long been a fan of Larry Crabb's in that I have read several of his books over the years and have been impressed with the way he always gets to the spiritual roots of our problems. I have found him to be a radical Christian—which in my mind is what we should all be if we are to come into all that Christ intends for us.

CHAPTER THREE

THE EXCHANGED LIFE

The only way we will be able to move from a natural ministry into a supernatural one is if we are willing to exchange our life for the life of Christ. This is a process that takes time, but if we are willing, Jesus Christ Himself will accomplish this in us.

This is God's plan for every Christian—that we would decrease in order that He may increase in us. He wants to live His life in us in order to reveal Himself to a lost and dying world. He desires to become one with us, even as a bridegroom and his bride become one, each retaining his/her own identity but becoming one.

According to the Bible, humankind is tripartite having a spirit, soul and body. We see this in Paul's prayer in I Thessalonians 5:23: *And the very God of peace sanctify you wholly; and I pray God your whole spirit and soul and body be preserved blameless unto the coming of our Lord Jesus Christ.*

When we are born again, the Holy Spirit comes to reside within our spirit. It is with our spirit that we are able to commune with God and fellowship with Him. In our spirit we hear His still small voice as He guides us, teaches us, and comforts us. We have the mind of Christ in our spirit; therefore, we want to be led by our spirit as we minister and as we conduct our daily lives.

We also have a soul in which resides our natural mind. Our natural mind wants to take the lead and do things according to our own reasoning and understanding. God tells us in Isaiah 55:8,9: *For my thoughts are not your thoughts, neither are your ways my ways, saith the LORD. For as the heavens are higher than the earth, so are my ways higher than your ways, and my thoughts than your thoughts.*

T. Austin Sparks explains:

Whether we are able yet to accept it or not, the fact is that if we are going on with God fully, all the soul's energies and abilities for knowing, understanding, sensing and doing will come to an end...But what joy and strength there is when, the soul having been constrained to yield to the spirit, the higher wisdom and glory is perceived in its vindication...So that unto fullness of joy the soul is essential, and it must be brought through the darkness and death of its own ability to learn the higher and deeper realities for which the spirit is the first organ and faculty. (Sparks)

The problem with our own thoughts and our own ways is that they are always mixed with impure motives derived from our self-nature. Jeanne Guyon expressed it quite well when she wrote:

There is something in this universe which is the very opposite of God; it is the self. The activity of the self is the source of all the evil nature as well as all the evil deeds of man...As long as you employ your self-nature in any way, some faults will also continue to exist in you. But after you depart from your selfhood, no faults can exist, and all is purity and innocence. (Guyon, 126)

46

We are not able to think God's thoughts in purity in our soul because of this mixture. Our carnal motives are usually hidden from us until the Holy Spirit reveals them. He reveals them to us so we can repent of them and ask Him to remove them. Most often the way God removes them is by taking us through a painful experience, as He burns away the sin nature and purifies an area of our soul. When an area of our soul is purified, it comes under the control of the spirit. Once that area comes under the control of our spirit, which is united with the Holy Spirit, then God can pour Himself into that area and use it to His glory.

Watchman Nee states that our soul and spirit are like the grain of wheat that must fall into the ground and die if we are to bring forth fruit (John 12:24). Our spirit is the inner part of the grain, and the outer shell represents our soul that must be broken before the inner life of the spirit can pour forth in ministry to others. It is God who must break that outer soul-ish life in us and this can take a number of years to accomplish.

> The Lord employs two different ways to break our outward man (soul); one is gradual, the other sudden. To some, the Lord gives a sudden breaking followed by a gradual one. With others, the Lord arranges that they have constant daily trials, until one day He brings about large-scale breaking. If it is not the sudden first and then the gradual, then it is the gradual followed by the sudden. It would seem the Lord usually spends several years upon us before He can accomplish this work of breaking. (Nee 1965, 14)

If we are to minister effectively to satanically ritually abused persons, we have to be willing for God to break us so that His Spirit can flow out of us to accomplish the ministry. If we co-operate with Him, this breaking can be accomplished more quickly. One hindrance to this work of God in our lives is our ignorance of the ways in which He works. Too often we view trials as coming from Satan to hinder us, when actually they are God's tools for refining and purifying our lives. The great 17th century Christian, Francois de Fenelon wrote, "Slowly you will learn that all the troubles in your life—your job, your health, your inward failings—are really cures to the poison of your old nature" (Fenelon, 23).

To illustrate, I would like to share how God called me into the SRA ministry and brought me through a painful experience in order to burn away my own selfish motives and purify the ministry. Everyone who wants to minister in God's strength and power will probably have to go through a comparable trial for the ministry to be cleansed.

One day in 1992 I received a phone call from a friend who knew a lot of people came to me for help with their problems. She said the Lord had prompted her to call me and suggest that I read a book concerning how to minister to SRA persons. I had never heard of satanic ritual abuse, but knowing that this woman heard from God, I immediately bought the book and read it. Shortly after reading the book I began seeing announcements on Christian television advertising a seminar on SRA that was to be held in Columbus, OH by the author of the book I had just read. While driving my car, I turned on the radio just as the announcement was being made about this seminar. A brochure about it came to me in the mail.

I began to wonder if the Lord might be telling me to go to this seminar, but decided it was impossible. The seminar was on Friday and Saturday, but I had college classes to attend Friday. I was determined not to miss any lectures. The next time I attended class, I learned that the entire university would be closed down that particular Friday because of winter break! My first thought was, "Wow, Lord! You shut down the whole university just so I could attend that seminar!"

After attending the seminar I decided I was ready to minister so I prayed and asked the Lord to send someone who was SRA to me for help. I didn't have long to wait...!

A friend of mine worked for an organization that helps handicapped persons. While in the home of one of these persons, she began to notice that this particular woman seemed to have emotional problems. She suggested that the woman call me, which she did. During my second visit to her home, a little child alter popped up and began talking to me about how she had to polish all the crosses and candlesticks before the satanic rituals. God had answered my prayer.

God did not bring just one SRA person to me; over the next few months several more appeared at my door--some from our own church and some from the community. I found myself totally engrossed in a fascinating and difficult ministry. As I ministered I learned increasingly to draw upon the Lord for His strength, His understanding and His power. There were many occurrences for which the seminar had not prepared me. From time to time I would call others in SRA ministry in other cities for help. They often had no answers for me. My only recourse was to depend more upon the Lord and do whatever it seemed He was leading me to do.

God was definitely blessing the ministry. Through reliance upon the Holy Spirit I was able to manage every difficult alter, break the most complex programming and cast out every demon that manifested. It was after about two years that the trouble began...

Some people in the church complained that I was not qualified nor competent to minister in this field of SRA. The husband of one of the women in our church to whom I was ministering decided his wife was not satanically ritually abused. He called a national Christian ministry and told them about me. They assured him that I had no business trying to minister to SRA persons.

I had always respected this organization. How could they say such a thing when they did not know me or anything about my ministry except what this man said? I was crushed.

Then he gave us an ultimatum: either I quit this ministry or he and his family and friends would leave the church. My husband, as pastor of the church, stood by me through this entire trial and affirmed me in my calling and ministry. He assured them that I would not discontinue the ministry. The man followed through on his threat and left the church taking several family members and friends with him. Our church was not large so their leaving was evident to everyone. Eventually others also left, not because of this issue, but just because they saw other people leave.

The person most deeply hurt through all this was the satanically ritually abused woman to whom I ministered. There is not the slightest doubt that she was ritually abused. I had met several child alters and also an alter that could only bark like a dog. She had abreacted (experienced cognitive, emotional, and physical memory all together) in front of me several times. Notwithstanding, when one does not want to believe it could happen in THEIR family and when a nationally acclaimed ministry endorses one's stand, truth can be cast aside.

Some may ask, Wouldn't other persons also see this in her and eventually confirm my conclusion? My answer is, probably not, for three reasons. First, the satanically ritually abused are, without a doubt, the most abused, hurting people on earth. God is most protective of them. Many of the women whom I have taken through their memories into wholeness had been seen by several mental health professionals and even hospitalized without the issue of SRA ever having been exposed. I believe this is because God keeps it hidden until someone is present who understands the spiritual issues associated with Satanism and can bring the Holy Spirit into the ministry.

Second, few professional counselors are looking for it. Satanic ritual abuse and the resultant multiple personality disorders are considered extremely rare by the counseling community at large.

Third, God is able to set certain limits upon the alters and demons in an SRA person who is committed to Jesus Christ. If no one is available to minister them through to wholeness, God can enable them to function reasonably well if their abuse was not extreme. When I say "function reasonably well," I mean they may not experience a mental breakdown but they certainly won't be able to enjoy the freedom and joy that comes with wholeness in Jesus Christ. They will definitely experience emotional problems but the SRA aspects will remain hidden.

I had experienced numerous trials throughout our many years of pastoring churches, but this was the most painful. There was a pain deep inside that kept me awake nights crying. It took months for the pain to leave. As I suffered through this trial, I knew that God had allowed it for a reason. I was well acquainted with the principle of the cross—that all things, even good things, must die and be resurrected in order to be purified.

This ministry had to go through the cross in order to be cleansed from the mixed motives behind it. This is true of every ministry. We minister from our soul until we die to the ministry—that is until God burns away our impure motives and leaves the ministry purified for His use. It is just at this juncture that many become discouraged and leave their calling, whether it be pastoral ministry or some other kind of ministry. The church, for the most part, has failed to teach people about the way of the cross, and because of this, many don't understand God's purpose in their trials.

What were the impure motives I had connected to the SRA ministry? There were probably some of which I am not aware, but I do believe that I was allowing the ministry to give me a sense of self-worth. I felt I was a person of value because of the successes evident in the ministry and the dimension of spirituality affiliated with it.

All human beings have a deeply rooted need to know that they have worth and value—that their life counts for something. All of us have things we do in life to fulfill that need. Whatever we do well will become our way of fulfilling that desire; however, this is sin. God wants us to know that we have worth and value because He died for us and loves us. When we use anything other than God for satisfying this desire, it becomes an idol.

Looking back over my life, I can see that this need to prove that I had value was a driving force behind most of my activities and endeavors. My prayer for years was, "O God, please don't let me be just a pastor's wife. I want a ministry." I was always involved in the work of our church but never felt I had a ministry of my own. After several years of trials, the Lord brought me to a place where I was able to say from the bottom of my heart, "Lord, knowing You makes me so happy I don't care if I ever have a ministry. I'm content to be at home keeping house, cooking meals and loving my husband." A few days after this prayer, desperate people started knocking on my door seeking help, and they continue to do so to this day. God knew, and was showing me, that He had first place in my heart. Then, and only then, would He permit my ministry (and His) to begin.

God loves us so much He wants to make sure that He holds first place in our heart before He allows us to enter deeply into our calling. Misunderstanding this has been, I believe, the cause of the fall of many large ministries. When the ministry has first place in our heart, we're in trouble, and the ministry will eventually fail. No matter how desperate the plight of the people I help, God always lets me know that His first concern is for me and our relationship. I sense the jealousy of His love and it fills my heart with unspeakable joy. Never, never, never will He permit anyone or any ministry to supersede our relationship!

Along with my impure motive of needing to find worth and value in my ministry was also the deeply rooted concern over what other people thought of me. Most of us, to one degree or another, base much of our self-worth on what we perceive others think about us. This was an extremely painful death for me. The whole church and others in the community knew of this issue and were talking about me. Those who were criticizing me were free to express themselves, but I was bound by confidentiality to my abused friend. I could not ethically defend myself based upon what I had seen and heard. All I could do was be silent and depend upon God to defend me if He chose to do so.

As God took me through this trial, He also dealt with my natural curiosity. When one ministers in the area of SRA, one sees and hears many astonishing and mystifying things. Questions arise in the spiritual helper's mind demanding answers that no textbook can give. Even the Bible seems to be silent concerning many things seen and heard in these ministry sessions. Before dying to the ministry, the temptation may arise to ask the wounded person questions to satisfy one's curiosity that may not necessarily be in the person's best interests. Once God puts this curiosity through His refining fire, the temptation will no longer persist.

The Lord is now free to bless our newly refined curiosity as He chooses. It has been my experience that as I rest in Him, He delights in explaining things to me. One way He often blesses me is through those to whom I am giving spiritual direction. When the Lord comes to minister His presence to them after their memories, He sometimes also has a special word for me.

Another way He satisfies my curiosity is through His written Word. The deeper I go into the SRA ministry, the deeper He takes me into His Word. The deeper I go into His Word, the deeper He takes me into the SRA ministry. He has blessed me with many golden nuggets of beautiful truth hidden beneath the surface of His word. God loves our curiosity, but it must be separated from our impure motives before He can fully bless it.

A word of caution...one should never seek to satisfy one's curiosity about the cults by delving into occult books. I consider this to be a waste of time, and it definitely exposes one to the deceiving spirits of darkness.

At the same time that people were criticizing me and leaving the church, God was confirming my calling with some of the most amazing and supernatural things I'd ever seen. My power over the demons was increasing. God was giving me more innovative ways of dealing with alters and deeper revelations of the inner worlds of abused persons.

By persevering through the trial, I died to the ministry as God removed the impure motives connected to it. The ministry was no longer coming forth from my soul but it had come under the dominance of my spirit that was joined to the Holy Spirit. This is not to say the ministry was absolutely perfect, but I had progressed into a new dimension of ministry and a deeper intimacy with Christ.

CHAPTER FOUR

THE PRINCIPLE OF AUTHORITY

The centurion answered and said, Lord, I am not worthy that thou shouldest come under my roof: but speak the word only, and my servant shall be healed. For I am a man under authority, having soldiers under me: and I say to this man, Go, and he goeth; and to another, Come, and he cometh; and to my servant, Do this, and he doeth it.

When Jesus heard it, he marvelled, and said to them that followed, Verily I say unto you, I have not found so great faith, no, not in Israel.

As we minister to bring people out of the darkness of occult bondage it is necessary that we deal with demonic spirits. To be successful in this endeavor it is imperative that we understand the principle of authority. The entire spirit realm of the evil supernatural and the good supernatural operates under the principle of authority.

We read in Ephesians 6:12: *For we wrestle not against flesh and blood, but against principalities, against powers, against the rulers of the darkness of this world, against spiritual wickedness in high places.* This scripture is teaching us that our enemy is not man but the spiritual forces behind man. As America plunges more and more into the occult darkness of this present age, it will become increasingly important that we understand and utilize this principle.

We used to be able to solve problems through the established systems of our culture such as the courts, the educational system, government agencies, etc. These institutions served us well when America operated more or less under the Judeo-Christian principles embraced by our founding fathers. However, as lawlessness has prevailed and the so-called restraints of Christianity have been cast aside, these agencies today often assist the evildoer while the righteous person is condemned. What used to be taken for granted as common sense no longer prevails in our land.

Many Christians agree we are living in the time of the harvest. We will be seeing more and more the fullness of evil being manifested in our nation and around the world. Simultaneously God will be manifesting his holiness, love and awesome power through His people who have chosen to die to self and live unto Him. The struggle between good and evil is becoming increasingly obvious. As this battle intensifies, we will be called upon to abandon our old ways of fighting in the natural and enter into the greatest spiritual warfare of all time.

Leaders who are instruments of unrighteousness have risen to positions of power and prestige all over this nation. Many of these people understand full well the realm of the supernatural. The power necessary to rise to high places of authority and influence has been gained by many through the use of evil supernatural powers gained through satanic rituals. What do you think these people are doing the night before an important election? They're involved in powerful rituals sending forth the demons of hell into our population to influence the voters' minds. What do you think the average Christian is doing the night before a big election? Probably sitting at home watching television. The power released through the prayers of the righteous far exceeds the power sent forth through satanic rituals, but few Christians are praying with the fervor displayed by the wicked.

Why are the wicked so willing to sacrifice their time and effort to gain power while so many Christians slumber in their easy chairs before the TV? The answer lies in the difference between the Devil's *modus operandi* and God's. The Devil drives people by force and duress. They are compelled and driven to do what they do. God gently woos us with His love but never compels or forces us to follow Him. If we don't want a relationship with God, He isn't going to force us into one. That would have no meaning to Him. God created us for relationship with Himself, but that relationship is meaningless unless we freely choose Him.

In addition to this, the deeds of darkness appeal to the sin nature in man. The things of God are more difficult requiring self-denial and faith. God always asks us to do that which seems the opposite of our natural reasoning, such as forgiving our enemies. Getting revenge on our enemies, the tactic of the Devil, appeals more to our natural instincts.

Those who choose to follow the Devil into occult and satanic practices are greatly deceived. Satan gives them rewards of power, money etc. for a season; however, Satan operates under the law of diminishing returns. There may come a time when the price for such benefits has increased to the point the person is no longer willing to pay. Millions who are ignorantly following after wickedness are going to wake up some day to realize they are in deep bondage and oppression, and there is no way out. At this point many will begin to cry out to the One True God for help and deliverance. This will necessitate turning to the church. These people will need deliverance and the church must be prepared to help them.

Understanding the principle of authority will be vital in bringing deliverance to those in bondage to the Devil. As we have seen in the passage from Matthew at the beginning of this section, one must be under authority in order to have authority. Jesus Christ came to this earth under the authority of His Father. The centurion recognized this as an important principle relating it to his own position in the military. He knew because he was under the authority of the one over him, he could direct those under him and they would do as he said.

As spiritual helpers it is imperative that we be under the authority of those God has placed over us. As a wife I am under the authority of my husband. That doesn't mean that he orders me around. It means that in my heart I am willing to let him take the lead in our home, and I trust God to bless me through my husband's leadership. This requires faith. I confess that I have not always thought my husband's decisions were perfectly right; however, he is a godly man, and I have learned to trust that God will bless me through his decisions. If I disagree with my husband concerning a certain matter, I usually tell him my viewpoint and leave it at that. Too often wives try to be the Holy Spirit directing their husbands in matters best left up to God.

I confess I have been guilty of this at times. Several years ago I remember being concerned about a certain issue in which I felt my husband needed to change. I tried my best to get him to follow my "excellent" counsel, but he wasn't interested. This had caused a little tension between us one particular evening. That night God gave me a dream. In my dream, my husband was lying on an operating table prepared for open-heart surgery. I was dressed in the usual operating room garb with my arms held up in the post scrub position asking for a scalpel. As I began to make the first incision, I suddenly realized I was no surgeon and hadn't a clue as to how to proceed. I got the message! I need to leave such matters in God's hands. He can do a much better job than I.

When wives try to tell their husbands what to do, it often causes only friction and discord in the marriage. That well-known passage concerning women in 1 Timothy 2:12 comes to mind. *But I suffer not a woman to teach, nor to usurp authority over the man, but to be in silence.* The Greek word for man here is *aner*. This word may be translated *husband* or *man*. The decision is up to the translators. *Aner* occurs 212 times in the New Testament. Sometimes it is translated *man* and sometimes *husband*. I prefer the rendering *husband* in this passage. It does not go well in a marriage for a woman to attempt to teach her husband; however, in the church, women can and do instruct men. Even in the New Testament there are accounts of women pastors.

Many times in the church I have heard Christian women complain that they could not submit to an "unsaved" husband. Numerous times when I heard about the particular situation, I thought the man had the wisdom. We need to trust that God will lead us through the authority figure He has put over us.

Another authority figure would be a pastor. We need to be under the covering of a godly pastor and the government of the church. Everyone needs to be under the authority of someone else. A submissive heart provides a covering and protection for us in the spiritual realm. To begin to walk in rebellion to authority is to open oneself for demonic oppression.

Just as the spiritual director needs to be under authority, the person needing deliverance from darkness must be submitted under the authority of the spiritual director. This is extremely important. The abused person will be under heavy pressure from the demons to follow their instructions. These instructions may be actual voices that the person hears or they may seem like his/her own thoughts. Either way, the demons' demands will be the opposite of the spiritual director's wisdom. The satanically ritually abused person is used to hearing and obeying the demons. To suddenly renounce these voices and obey the instructions of the spiritual director is most difficult.

When necessary God will lead the helper in establishing authority, and this needs to be accomplished as soon as possible or there will be very little progress in the survivor. Often an issue will arise that will cause a crisis which will not be resolved until the authority issue is settled. For example, I was helping a woman who had obviously been severely ritually abused and I was having difficulty handling the demons that kept surfacing in her. We weren't able to get much memory work done because of the constant interference of the demons that kept her almost hysterical. I had told her she needed to be on some sort of antidepressant. She had refused.

The satanically ritually abused frequently refuse to take any medication because they were often drugged by their abusers. I couldn't make any progress with her and finally told her that unless she started on a mild antidepressant, I was not going to work with her. This was the crisis that was needed. She called me the next day and said she had called her doctor and he had prescribed the antidepressant. We began working again, and I now had the authority over the demons. The mild antidepressant wasn't controlling the demons, my God-given authority was. Once the issue of authority was settled, she was able to progress beautifully through her memories and receive her subsequent healing.

Establishing authority through a crisis situation requires faith on the part of the spiritual helper and the survivor. I cared deeply for this woman who refused to take the antidepressant. I didn't want to lose her. I knew I could help her, and I knew that the psychiatric community had not. In the past she had been hospitalized in psychiatric wards, locked up in a padded cell and heavily sedated. She was diagnosed schizophrenic and as having a borderline personality disorder. I knew that spiritual ministry was her only hope.

This was a situation in which God led me through the one in authority over me—my husband, who also happens to be my pastor. He told me he didn't want me to minister to her anymore unless she took the medication. We also submitted this to a couple visiting in our home from another state. I had led this woman through her SRA memories a few years prior to this, so she and her husband understood what was transpiring. Everyone agreed that I needed to give her this ultimatum. Had I not been under authority, I don't know that I would have been able to make this difficult decision. My love and concern for her may have kept me from doing what needed to be done.

This had been my first experience with the principle of establishing authority with a survivor. Not long after that, the issue arose again, and because I understood the principle, I was able to approach the situation more directly. It is an interesting story.

I had been trying to help a woman through her SRA memories for almost two years. She would have one or two memories and then stop all ministry saying that she "made it all up." Then she would try again and, after a few memories, quit. I tried everything I knew to convince her that her memories were valid, but she chose not to submit to my authority. The problem was that when she was with me, she knew what was transpiring was valid, but when she left my presence, the voices of the demons would overpower what she knew to be true. Because she had not submitted to me, she listened to the voices rather than to me.

She had experienced cognitive, emotional and body memory all at the same time (abreaction). In my presence she had a memory of giving birth to a baby that was sacrificed when she was a young teen (not an uncommon memory). As the memory progressed, she went through the pain of labor in my presence. I watched as she cradled the baby in her arms, and I heard her screams and cries as it was taken from her and sacrificed. She even experienced the pain of her breasts filling with milk as the memory progressed. Many times Jesus Christ had come to her after a memory and given her great peace and healing for a memory. However, she again withdrew from our regular meetings saying her memories had come from her wicked imagination.

To begin SRA ministry and then withdraw before the memories are finished invites severe demonic oppression. We read in *Matthew 12:43-45: When the unclean spirit is gone out of a man, he walketh through dry places, seeking rest, and findeth none. Then he saith, I will return into my house from whence I came out; and when he is come, he findeth it empty, swept, and garnished. Then goeth he, and taketh with himself seven other spirits more wicked than himself, and they enter in and dwell there: and the last state of that man is worse than the first.*

This happened to this woman. She couldn't sleep. She heard doors opening and closing and footsteps in her house when no one was there. Oppression of every kind dominated her life after she quit seeking ministry. I was careful to maintain a relationship with her during this time. I was not able to help her because she wouldn't come under my authority, but I believed that at some point, when she was ready, we would continue ministry.

Then a health issue arose. She developed a severe cough while on a vacation with her sister at a ski resort in the mountains. Some of the decorations were of a psychic nature—signs of the Zodiac, tarot cards, and even a Ouija board. There was an antique radio there that was, for some reason, frightening to my friend. Her sister turned it on, and instantly my friend felt a demon enter her chest from the radio. That was when the coughing began, and it continued unabated for three months.

The cough was extremely severe to the point she was unable to attend church or talk on the telephone. This effectively cut off our communication. She even lost her voice for a few weeks. When her voice returned, she was still coughing several times in each sentence. She was unable to sleep more than a few minutes at a time, and the sleep of the entire family was disrupted every night.

She went to the doctor as a last resort (she is deathly afraid of doctors) and took an antibiotic that didn't help. There came a point, after much suffering, that she admitted to me over the phone that she felt the cough was demonic. She told me for the first time about the demon coming out of the radio into her chest. As she talked, a plan began to form in my mind. This could be our issue for establishing authority.

I prayed for her cough over the phone with no results. (I am often able to cast out demons over the telephone.) Then I suggested that I come to her house the next day to pray for her. She readily agreed.

The next day at her home I prayed for her to be delivered of the cough to no avail. Then I suggested that we submit a test before the Lord that would determine once for all whether her memories were true or false. It would also determine whether or not she would submit to the authority God had placed over her in her husband and her pastor and me. (Her husband, her pastor [my husband] and I had all agreed that her memories had been valid. She had refused to submit to any of us.) She agreed.

I sat at her kitchen table and wrote out a contract for her to sign. The contract went something like this: I, Susan Survivor (not a real name, of course), declare that I will submit to the authority of my husband, my pastor, and my healing prayer minister. I believe that my memories have been true, and I have not been making them up. Of my own free will I choose to serve the Lord Jesus Christ, and I renounce the Devil and all his demons.

I explained to her that if she signed this contract, she would be announcing to the demonic realm that she had chosen to submit herself to godly authority. If God then healed her of the cough, He would be validating that her memories are true and that He wanted her to come under our authority for her protection. This would settle the issue once and for all. She agreed and signed the contract.

I again prayed for her to be healed, and the demons began pouring out of her. The coughing ceased, and the Lord ministered to her by His presence. I remained in her home for about an hour as we sat around the kitchen table talking. She never coughed one time while I was there and she was able to converse freely. The authority issue was settled, and she made an appointment for the following week to begin ministry for healing again.

There is no doubt about the fact that establishing authority will enable the minister to be more effective in helping the survivor. I am reminded of a story about a very wise dentist. He was trying to work on the teeth of a little girl who was not cooperating with him. Finally, he turned to the girl's mother and asked her to come with him to the next room for a short conference. Out of the child's hearing he asked the mother if she would be willing to obey him in a few simple instructions in front of the girl. The mother agreed. They returned to the room where the little girl was waiting in the dentist's chair. The dentist then instructed the mother to do a few simple tasks, which she immediately did. The little girl was able to perceive that the dentist was the one in authority. She then cooperated with the dentist in all his instructions, and the work was completed.

CHAPTER FIVE

THE PURPOSE BEHIND SATANIC RITUAL ABUSE

In this chapter I will not be discussing Satanism as a whole but specifically Satanism as it pertains to the ritually abused. This kind of Satanism is often, but not always, passed down in families from generation to generation. If the abusers are not family members, they will be persons who have regular access to the child such as godparents or a babysitter.

Often, the ritually abused child is born into a family in which everyone is enslaved to the Devil either willingly or against their will. Because all family members are involved--grandparents, aunts, uncles, etc--there is absolutely no escape for a child. The cult family may be living in a cult community or cult town. There are small towns in rural areas in which almost everyone is involved in the cult to some extent. In this scenario there is virtually no one a child can access for help.

Another reason there is no way out for a ritually abused child is she is purposely kept in a state of deep confusion. She is not allowed to form a healthy identity. The pain and terror of the brutality she faces on a daily basis has necessitated her dissociating repeatedly to the point she has no idea who she is. She may not know what she is--whether she is a human, an animal, a machine, a male, a female, a ghost, a demon, a space alien, etc. She has been rendered virtually helpless by the abuse.

Amazingly with all this confusion, she is able to function and appear normal to the casual observer. Children with the ability to dissociate to the point of totally forgetting what happened tend to be exceptionally bright and talented children.

The number one reason people worship the Devil is to gain power--power to get rich, power to control others, power to be admired, power to get revenge, power to rule, power to bring in the reign of the Antichrist, etc. In Satanism, powers are demons and demons are powers. Cultists do rituals to get as many demons into themselves as possible. The powers they obtain from a ritual give them temporary powers or a temporary high. It is necessary to continually do more rituals in order to get the powers (demons).

At this point I would like to give an example of satanic power that I happened to see on television a few nights ago. Most people would not recognize what I am about to describe as being satanic power. I recognize it only because of the many ritual memories I've heard from survivors.

On this program a young magician was performing magic tricks. He had a young woman from the audience come on stage and select a card from a deck and show it to the audience (he, of course, not knowing what it was) and replace it in the deck. He then proceeded to blow up a very long, skinny balloon which he tied in knots until it resembled a sword. Taking this balloon sword he made one sweeping motion and cut a wooden table in two. At that point most people were probably thinking the table had been precut and only needed a touch to make it fall apart. Then he threw an apple into the air and cut it in half with the balloon sword. Okay, the apple could have been precut too. But then he threw the deck of cards into the air and pierced through one card with the end of the balloon in mid air. This created a large hole about two inches in diameter in the middle of the card through which the balloon protruded about three inches. That card was the one the girl had chosen. That was satanic power in action. That was totally impossible.

It is important for us to understand that Satan will not allow a man, or possibly a woman (most often they are men) perpetrator, to possess within himself/herself great powers. The powers are instilled through rituals into a victim from whom the perpetrator accesses the powers.

An infant is chosen, often in the womb, to be the "special" or "chosen" one to whom has been given the "honor" of being dedicated to Satan. She is subjected to hideous, painful rituals that cause demons to come into her. Those wanting to have the power must rape the child (or if the abuser is a woman, perform some other perverted sexual act) to gain the powers they desire. The demons are transferred from one person to another through sexual acts.

This "special" child will be abused for her powers throughout her entire life. Every kind of mind control imaginable is used to keep her totally controlled, confused and weak. Cultists purposely submit the child to tortures so severe that in order to survive she must dissociate. According to *Webster's New World College Dictionary* dissociation is *a split in the conscious process in which a group of mental activities breaks away from the main stream of consciousness and functions as a separate unit, as if belonging to another person.* This is what I will be referring to as splitting.

The most gifted child is the one with the greatest ability to dissociate. Cultists know full well that she is dissociating and are masters at devising ever-increasing acts of barbarism to cause her to split. Why do they want her to split? First, to keep her confused and unable to form an identity so she will be easier to control. Second, alters (dissociated personalities) can be programmed to do certain jobs to serve the cult's purposes. These alters can be accessed by the cult according to certain codes. Third, the more "persons" she becomes, the more demons can be attached to each one. The survivor who can switch the most will be the most valuable because she will have the most demons (powers).

Spiritual power comes from only two sources—Jesus Christ or Satan. God gives power to overcome all sin and temptation by giving His Holy Spirit to those who believe in the atoning sacrifice of His Son Jesus Christ. Persons involved in the darkness of the occult receive power from demons. In the Satanic cult world, demons are powers. If someone were to say, I have the power of extra sensory perception, they would be saying, I have the demon of extra sensory perception. Humans don't have spiritual powers. Powers come from spirit beings. The more demons one has, the more powers are available for achieving one's own selfish interests. The greatest powers (demons) must come through the heinous practice of satanic ritual abuse (SRA).

The child chosen to be the "special one" through whom the cultists will be able to receive power must become a living sacrifice. To receive power there must always be a sacrifice; it is a kingdom principle. Jesus Christ was the perfect sacrifice given once and for all, and by believing in Him, Christians receive power to overcome and live a victorious Christian life. However, this power is only accessible to us if we are willing to live according to God's instructions including Romans 12:1 where we are told to "...present your bodies a living sacrifice, holy, acceptable to God, which is your reasonable service." Most persons knowing anything about Satan worship have heard about sacrificing babies to Satan by murdering them. However, few have heard of the concept of the living sacrifice demanded by Satan.

God commands Christians to become living sacrifices unto Him. No Satan worshipper would be willing to be a living sacrifice for anyone because the very essence of Satanism is based on selfishness and greed; but in order to gain power, there must be a living sacrifice. Therefore, a helpless infant or child is chosen to be the living sacrifice unto Satan. The child is subjected to numerous painful and terrifying rituals whereby demons are summoned to come into the child making her a literal storehouse or battery of satanic powers that can be accessed by the cult members at will. The most common way these powers are accessed is by performing acts of sexual perversion on the child. The child, of course, grows up and matures into an adult but because of the severity of the abuse and psychological programming, often never realizes she possesses these powers. She suffers continual lifelong abuse from the demons, internal abusive programming, and the perpetrators themselves. This person has become a living sacrifice unto Satan and her life is a living hell.

What a heinous perversion of a glorious scriptural truth intended by God to draw His people into a close, loving relationship with Himself and thereby fill their lives with blessings!

It should be obvious by now that it requires spiritual ministry to minister to the satanically ritually abused and this involves casting out demons. The greatest psychological techniques and expertise known to man could never deliver another person from the torment caused by indwelling demon spirits. Only Christians empowered by the Holy Spirit have the discernment and power to deliver suffering people from the torment of demons.

Our power over these entities is directly commensurate to the degree to which we have been willing to die to self and allow Christ to fill us with more of Himself. If we are willing to be a living sacrifice unto God, we will have the love and power to deliver those who, against their will, were made living sacrifices unto Satan.

Because this kind of abuse is often carried on in families, they are able to have unlimited access to the child. The abuse occurs not only in rituals but also in daily family life. The child is not allowed to receive any love or affirmation. Mother is forbidden to hold her or comfort her. Dissociation becomes the only coping mechanism known to the child.

In this environment it is possible for a person to split into thousands. There are many who would not believe this, but if one thinks about it logically it is very possible. What can a little girl do when her older brother rapes her and then mother beats her for "making her brother do it?" She can dissociate. Mother tells the daughter she never wanted her because all she ever does is cause trouble (rape) in the family. Mother then lavishes affection on the brother who perpetrated the attack. The only way the little girl knows to cope is to switch and withdraw into an inner world of make-believe and demon friends. (Demon friends are explained in Chapter 12, Dealing with Demons.)

Rapes, beatings, false accusations, absence of love, are only some of the painful aspects for the satanically ritually abused child in a cult family. Her only recourse is to split. Rituals occur on a regular basis--probably at least once a week. There are certain special seasons of the year when rituals are performed every night for a week or more. The child may need to split into three or four alters just to get through one ritual. When this continues year in and year out, the alters do add up to thousands in the most severe cases.

The following is an example of one cult family described to me through the memories of one brutally abused woman. Keep in mind that the entire family understood the way to access her powers was through rape. The more they could torture her, the more she would split and the more powers she would have. Of course, everyone wanted her powers. She was kept so confused she didn't know anything about a cult or her powers. She dissociated so well she was able to forget all the rituals. One difficult aspect for her of having her memories was realizing that when she was a child the "whole town" knew of her involvement yet she was completely ignorant of it. It made her feel like a fool.

This dear woman had a father, three brothers, seven uncles and their wives, and a grandfather all who wanted her powers. She happened to live in a small, rural mountain town where almost everyone in town was in the cult. Some of those who availed themselves of her powers were the doctor, the dentist, the school principal, school teachers, music teacher, bus driver, the sheriff, two undertakers, etc. The list seems endless. Then she was sold to certain groups who would take her away to other towns. It seems that when one is as gifted as this, word gets around in the cult world. The family was able to make money "renting" her to groups for her powers.

Several times she was forced to attend conventions of magicians. When the convention ended for the day and most of the people left, this little girl was compelled to go through horrible rituals involving human sacrifice with a select group of magicians. The two highest bidders got to rape her to access her powers. It takes satanic powers to do some of the impossible magic "tricks" being seen on some television shows today. This kind of power is given only to a person who is willing to commit the most barbarous cruelty imaginable.

It seems to be a common practice in the cults that the most gifted SRA children are flown to other countries for intensive mind control and programming. The country most often mentioned in the memories of the people I have helped has been Germany. Many other countries have been named but Germany has been the most predominant. It is my opinion that Germany has been popular with cults because of the great darkness enveloping that area due to the death camps of WWII. Demons are territorial. They are the most powerful and prevalent in areas where there has been the greatest suffering and death. It is my contention that these children have been put through rituals there to bring the demons back to the United States. Certainly there have been terrible atrocities in other countries too, but with the cults there seems to be something special about Germany.

I believe that satanic ritual abuse also has something to do with bringing the Antichrist to power. The alters and demons speaking through SRA persons talk about the coming reign of Satan on earth through the Antichrist and his followers. Satanic ritual abuse seems to be a major way of obtaining the power to bring this to pass.

It would appear that the people with the greatest satanic powers, the kinds of powers that bring national and international recognition, have to access many SRA survivors for their powers. In other words, a man cannot rise to national prominence through satanic power by having one woman as his source of power. He needs to attend many rituals, offer many sacrifices and abuse many women and children to have that much power. For this reason, a spiritual helper who helps many survivors may hear certain names of abusers repeated by more than one woman.

Understanding the purpose behind satanic ritual abuse has not come easily to me as I have ministered to various SRA persons. They are so horribly abused and confused they don't understand why these things were done to them. Once in a while they appear to apprehend one or two aspects of it, but for the most part they are just innocent victims who are overwhelmed by the brutality and sadness of their lives. They know they were raped but many of them don't understand why. Knowing the purpose behind SRA helps the spiritual director discern when a ritual memory is coming to an end. (Rape comes at the end of a ritual.) It also aids in detecting SRA because if a woman is having many rape memories, it could be an indication that she may soon have ritual abuse memories.

The first abused woman I tried to help many years ago began having one rape memory after another. I was not her counselor; I was her friend but when she was with me the memories started popping up. I couldn't figure out why all these men had wanted to rape her. It just didn't make sense. Now I know--she must have been a survivor of satanic ritual abuse. They wanted her powers. At the time I had never heard of SRA and was not equipped to minister to her. She eventually was hospitalized for her emotional problems. I now suspect she was satanically ritually abused because of the many rape memories, her ability to see into the spiritual realm and the way demons acted out in her.

The manifestation of demons is a major tip-off to some kind of satanic involvement. During deliverance the demons would take over her body. They would speak through her. They would take over her hands and try to strangle her. When demons manifest so fully in a person, they have been given permission to do so either in satanic rituals or because a person knowingly invited them in to gain certain powers. At the time I had no idea God had called me into this ministry but I was getting a taste of how impossible it is to help these dear ones apart from the very presence and power of God.

Observers of Times

The Bible states in Deut. 18:10-12a: *There shall not be found among you any one that maketh his son or his daughter to pass through the fire, or that useth divination, or an observer of times, or an enchanter, or a witch, or a charmer, or a consulter with familiar spirits, or a wizard, or a necromancer. For all that do these things are an abomination unto the LORD.*

Making children pass through the fire is a reference to satanic ritual abuse. Sometimes children are burned to death in sacrifices. At other times the chosen SRA child is made to walk on hot coals as a demonstration of her powers. When her powers are great, she can walk on a bed of hot coals without being burned.

Rituals are commonly done at certain times when the satanic powers seem to be greatest. One of these times is the time of the full moon. It is no coincidence that schoolteachers notice their children act up more around that time of the month. Rituals are being done all over the world at the full moon to send forth demons to disrupt people's lives. This is a time when those who are SRA will feel a greater torment. They may feel strongly compelled to go out to a ritual or they may be more confused and emotional at this time. Demons may appear at their bedside at night to torment them and disrupt their sleep.

Rituals are commonly held on weekend nights no matter what the stage of the moon. They often begin around midnight and last until 3:00 or 4:00 A.M. However, a ritual can take place any time of the day or night. Satanists believe they have greater powers when certain astrological phenomena occur such as planetary alignments, spring and fall equinoxes, summer and winter solstices, eclipses, comets, meteor showers or any other unusual planetary occurrence.

Certain days are also believed to be more powerful—Friday the 13th for example. Or if certain numbers pertaining to the date occur in a particular order, their powers are supposed to be increased. For example, February 2, 2000 which would be 2-2-2 was to be a powerful day because 2+2+2=6, and 6 is one of the numbers of the Beast (666) in Revelation. They use addition and multiplication to come up with powerful numbers. Nineteen ninety-eight was to have been a powerful cult year because it was three (the number of the unholy trinity) times 666 (the number of the Beast) which equaled 1998. Sometimes one of these dates will coincide with a planetary phenomenon increasing their powers. There was one of these in 1998 when Friday the 13th occurred the same night as the full moon and a lunar eclipse.

Satanists also like to have rituals on holidays in order to desecrate whatever good thing the holiday is commemorating. Rituals held on Christian holidays are mockeries of Jesus Christ and all for which He stands. It is my understanding rituals done on Mother's Day and Father's Day are intended to tear down the family. Fourth of July rituals are meant to destroy patriotism and bring forth powers for One World Government, etc. A ritually abused person is subjected to a painful ritual on her birthday turning a day usually intended for joy into a day of pain and dread.

Certain ritual locations are favored by Satanists for the purposes of receiving and transmitting power. Historical places where massive numbers of people died such as the WWII concentration camps in Europe or certain battlegrounds are favorite places along with, of course, cemeteries. They like to receive spirits here and also send forth spirits to bring about similar devastations in current society. They also like places where there are manmade structures related to astrology such as Indian burial mounds laid out congruent to certain constellations or some of the more famous architectural feats related to astrology of previous centuries

Some ritual locations are chosen for the purpose of controlling the entity relative to the site. For example, to control education they would have rituals in schools or universities. To control government, they have rituals in government buildings, etc. Rituals can take place anywhere or anytime. Those who conduct them are in bondage to the Devil and are driven to participate in them regularly and frequently. For many it becomes their way of coping with life...their way of getting high...and there is seemingly no way out. The penalty for trying to leave some cults is to have the sexual organs cut off, the tongue cut out and other tortures performed that lead to a slow and painful death. This is one reason we don't hear much about what they do. The penalty for talking is too dear a price to pay, but we know that in Jesus Christ all things are possible for him who believes. Those who have been ritually abused have a special covering and grace for coming out. I believe it would be harder for a perpetrator to leave. People would be more likely to believe a perpetrator than a confused SRA survivor with multiple personalities. Therefore, his testimony would be more damaging to the cult.

CHAPTER SIX

GOALS FOR ABUSE MINISTRY

It is imperative for the spiritual director to understand there should be no rigid formula for ministering to persons who have suffered severe abuse. Each individual is unique and no two persons will respond exactly the same way. To enter into a ministry session with a predetermined agenda will limit the Holy Spirit's ability to bring total healing to the individual. Only God truly knows the individual and what happened to her. He alone knows exactly how this wounded person should be approached. We must be sensitive to the Holy Spirit and follow His guidance. However, we need to have a thorough understanding of the basic goals that need to be accomplished for the person's healing. How these goals are achieved is up to the Holy Spirit. Before enumerating these goals I would like to say a few things about memories.

In one sense DID/SRA persons are all alike...they are all desperately wounded people. Spiritual helpers must have Christ's love, gentleness and patience in abundance to avoid further wounding them. I have learned that great patience must be employed in each session. It may take months before trust is developed to the point the person is able to have her first memory. Some persons will be able to describe their memory as they are experiencing it. Others will not be able to verbalize their memory at first. I have had several occurrences where the person was obviously experiencing a painful memory but refused to tell me about it. When this happens they must gently be entreated to tell the memory. They need to understand as long as it remains unexpressed it will have a hold over them. The events of SRA and/or sexual abuse are so humiliating persons may fear you will no longer desire a relationship if you know what they were forced to do. It is helpful to explain to them they will be stuck in their memory until it is verbally expressed. Others will have a complete memory and tell every detail while releasing their emotions. This is much easier and facilitates the healing process.

Why, some may ask, is it necessary to remember the abuse? There are several reasons for this necessary prerequisite to healing. David said in Psalm 32:3-5 *When I kept silence, my bones waxed old through my roaring all the day long. For day and night thy hand was heavy upon me: my moisture is turned into the drought of summer. Selah. I acknowledged my sin unto thee, and mine iniquity have I not hid. I said, I will confess my transgressions unto the LORD; and thou forgavest the iniquity of my sin. Selah.* Abused persons were forced into situations where it was inevitable that they sin. No child subjected to sexual and physical abuse can help but harbor bitterness, unforgiveness, resentment, etc in his/her heart. When the abuse is totally buried these sins cannot be confessed and the abuser forgiven.

There is something about verbally expressing inner hurts and beliefs that brings healing and understanding. I remember one abused young man who was troubled by something he kept pondering in his mind. Finally one day he told me about this troubling thought. He thought that Satan was going to repent. Jesus would change His own name to Satan and be thrown into the lake of fire. After he told me this and we talked about it for a few minutes, he got a big grin on his face. After telling me his thought it seemed silly and he was laughing at himself for entertaining it.

Emotional pain is also buried with the memory and can cause depression and deep-seated feelings of shame for which the person can find no cause. All manner of fears, even panic attacks, may plague a person's life seemingly without a cause. During memory work the genesis of these troubling emotions can be uncovered and dealt with through prayer and learning the truth.

Vows were often made at the time of abuse. In Satanism children are forced repeatedly to vow allegiance to Satan and certain cult members. In addition to these vows, all of us as children make vows that become self-imposed curses. A common example of this type of vow would be: I will never trust anyone. The Bibles tells us in James 5:12: *But above all things, my brethren, swear not, neither by heaven, neither by the earth, neither by any other oath: but let your yea be yea; and your nay, nay; lest ye fall into condemnation.* Cult induced vows subject the abused person to cult control and demonic harassment. Inner vows, the kind all of us make at some time in childhood, also become curses that afflict our lives with re-peated disappointments and failures. All of these vows can be repented of and renounced at the time of the memory. John and Paula Sandford write about the inner vows we all make in childhood in their book, *The Transformation of the Inner Man.*

> An inner vow is a determination set by the mind and heart into all the being in early life. Vows we make currently also affect us, but an inner vow is one set into us as children, usually forgotten. Our inner be-ing persistently retains such programming no matter what changes of mind and heart may later pertain. The distinctive mark of an inner vow is that it resists the normal maturation process, "When I was a child, I used to speak as a child, think as a child, reason as a child; when I became a man, I did away with child-

ish things: (1 Cor. 13:11). We may have many childish peculiarities, but we mature and leave them behind, reminded only by friends, relatives, and family reminiscences. Normal childish proclivities do not harm us other than to embarrass or prevent us as children, goading us to mature, until we "do away with them"; i.e., shyness, awkwardness, absentmindedness, insensitivity toward others' feelings, etc. But inner vows resist change. We do not grow out of them. (Sandford 1982, 193)

As a child matures, his identity is formed through his experiences. When he repeatedly encounters abuse, he forms an abuse identity that locks him into an unhealthy self-concept. It is only through remembering his abuse that this unhealthy self-concept can be identified and replaced with a healthy biblical identity. This is a slow process and must progress memory by memory. The abuse identity explains why an abused woman returns to an abusive husband. She believes it is her role in life to be abused. When she is away from the abuse, she feels she has no identity and therefore returns to it.

It is vitally important for a memory to be thoroughly and completely resolved before the survivor leaves your presence. For this reason ministry sessions need to be as open ended as possible. Each person is different but probably at least two hours should be the minimum time allotted for a memory. For anyone to leave your presence without her memory being fully processed may endanger her greatly. For example if she leaves before releasing the anger aroused by the memory, she might later erupt in anger endangering another person or herself. Others might leave feeling suicidal and do themselves harm.

It has been my experience that successful ministry to severely abused persons requires laying one's own life on the altar to Christ. In our microwave, instant everything, push-button society we tend to want quick results with everything. We bristle if we have to wait in a supermarket line for five minutes. We are busy people with crowded schedules trying to cram as much as possible into each day. This mentality has even crept into abuse counseling theories with some making claims that DID/SRA can be successfully resolved in only a few months. In my opinion this is impossible and should not be attempted. When God calls us into this ministry (and only those called by Him should be involved) we should be willing to give as much of our time as necessary to bring someone to total healing. Those who advocate DID/SRA can be fully healed in a few months because the survivor doesn't have to experience every single memory may well have a limited understanding of the depth of some persons' abuse and of how the abuse identity needs to be slowly dismantled and a new identity built. The pain and anger of a lifetime of abuse cannot be released in a few months.

It is true that in DID/SRA not every incident of abuse needs to be remembered. It is true that alters can sometimes be dealt with in groups. Yes, Jesus does come and comfort them and show them the truth after each memory. However, this in no way means DID/SRA can be fully healed in a few months. It is my concern that this mentality will produce partially healed persons believing they are completely free of their abuse issues only to have them recur a year or two after "successfully completing their healing." This may result in hopelessness, despair or even suicide.

Abuse usually starts in infancy or when the child is very young and vulnerable. Most often the perpetrators are persons who have easy and regular access to the child such as parents or other relatives, live-in partners, daycare providers, nursery school or kindergarten workers, etc. Therefore, episodes of abuse are seldom few in number. Most likely the abuse will happen several times a week over a period of years.

It is easy for a counselor or spiritual helper to deal with a few memories, see the person improving and come to the conclusion the person is totally healed. Some have actually claimed that SRA can be healed in a few weeks or just a few hours! Those making these claims mean well and sincerely desire to help others, but they are deceived. These counselors are bringing the presence of Jesus to their counselees and are seeing definite victories but they mistakenly think that because Jesus has been present and dealt with some things that the healing is complete. However, there are three reasons why this is impossible.

The first reason is that the abuse is usually far more extensive than we would surmise. It is true that a person doesn't have to go through every single memory, but the fact is they have to experience a considerable number in order to be healed. This is because (reason #2) the emotional pain of their experience is still locked deep inside and needs to be released. The pain of SRA is horrendous. This pain needs to be released a little at a time, memory by memory, in order for the person to be thoroughly healed. Some memories are so very painful (such as the memory of giving birth to a baby that was sacrificed) that weeks of grieving must occur before the next memory is dealt with. People cannot be rushed through memories with this depth of pain. Neither can the unremembered incidents be considered healed just because a person prayed a certain prayer and experienced the Lord's presence. When memories are not dealt with, a person feels some of the unpleasant emotions of his/her experience but doesn't know why, and this causes depression and hopelessness.

I was never abused, but sometimes the Lord allows me to experience certain things to reinforce the validity of the concepts He is teaching me. I am basically a happy person, but one morning recently I felt tremendous joy as I was preparing for my day. I wondered why this deep effervescent joy was bubbling up so powerfully on that particular day. In answer to my question, the Lord brought to mind a dream I had experienced during the night. In my dream I was a small child holding onto a stuffed animal (one I remember well from childhood) and I was sobbing uncontrollably. Someone had hurt my feelings and the pain had remained locked inside all these years. Jesus released that pain and that is why I was so joyful that particular morning. Something that had diminished my joy had been removed as I experienced the healing of a childhood memory. If my joy could be diminished over such a small incident, think of the enormity of emotional neediness in the satanically ritually abused!

The third reason why SRA takes a long time to heal involves the abuse identity. During the years of childhood abuse, the person is attempting to form an authentic identity but the identity formed is all based on lies. These lies need to be identified, renounced and replaced with truth. This is a long process because we have to slowly dismantle the false identity and build a true identity in Jesus Christ.

These three aspects of SRA—its extensiveness, the depth of pain, and the abuse identity—make it clear that the effects of SRA take a long time to heal completely. There is nothing wrong with taking time for something so important to be done thoroughly. There is grave danger for those who have had small victories to believe they are healed and then experience the darkness coming over them again in a few months or a year. This can bring a sense of hopelessness greater than before.

Those persons whose childhood abuse was extremely severe but not satanic ritual abuse may have dissociated enough to form several alters...perhaps as many as fifty. But persons who were subjected to satanic ritual abuse all through childhood will have dissociated far more times. The number of alters created through this abuse may even be in the hundreds or possibly thousands. When abuse is constant in the home and rituals occur two or more times a week (it may take the creation of several alters to get through one ritual), it is easy to see that the number of alters formed can be manifold. These individuals will be highly complex in their system of alters, programming and demonic controls. I will be referring to these individuals as being highly complex.

The following is a list of basic goals that need to be accomplished for the complete healing of an abuse memory:

1. The abuse must be remembered.
2. The emotions resulting from the abuse must be released.
3. If necessary, the demons attached to the memory must be removed.
4. The lies believed because of the abuse must be exposed and replaced with truth.
5. The person must be comforted and reassured.
6. The person needs to choose to forgive the perpetrators and trust God to change his/her feelings.
7. Any other aspects of the abuse must be resolved i.e. vows renounced, curses broken, magic surgery devices removed, etc.
8. Alters need to be comforted, led to safety and/or merged.

These are goals that should be accomplished for a memory to be thoroughly resolved. The first six goals should be completed for any type of severe abuse. The last two will be necessary for completion of most SRA memories. Remember, these are goals rather than a formula so things may not always progress in this order. At this point I would like to elaborate on each goal.

Dissociative persons must have memories of their abuse in order to be healed but each person will progress differently.

Some will have a memory during each session. If complexity is extremely high, they may have more than one memory. Others will progress more slowly and won't have memories each time. If the individual is experiencing serious problems with daily living, some of these current issues will need to be resolved before memory work can continue. It is not unusual to experience a break in memory work for a period of a few weeks while these current issues are being settled. One memory may be expressed through several different alters. This will be covered more thoroughly in another chapter.

Usually some emotions are expressed during the course of the memory but after the memory there must be plenty of time for more emotions to be fully released. It is good to encourage the person to cry, scream and release anger. I keep a large foam pillow with a changeable pillowcase accessible. It is often helpful to place it on the person's lap and encourage her to beat on it to release anger. Some like to hold it up to their face and scream into it.

When emotions seem to be blocked or the person is fighting against releasing them, I have found some gesture of compassion and love often breaks the dam, for example a hug (if you know the person well and they are of the same sex), a gentle squeeze of the shoulder, or touching their hand. Abused persons often fear releasing emotions because they were severely punished for doing so in childhood. They are also afraid of losing control. They are experts in putting up defensive walls or stuffing their emotions. Love helps break down these defenses so emotions can be expressed.

When I lead a woman through DID/SRA memories (most of them are women), a deep friendship develops between us. Some of these ladies need to be held and comforted as a mother would comfort a child. When I used to minister to a man, my husband or another male member of our church staff would be present. Now my husband has joined me in the SRA ministry and he ministers to the men. This is good protection insuring that no one can accuse us of inappropriate behavior. Demons are very crafty and can cause an abused person to think something happened when it didn't. Not being alone with a member of the opposite has proved to be a good safeguard for us in ministry.

Releasing of painful emotions will hopefully occur during the memory and then for another day or two depending on the severity of the memory and the individual. Some memories will need a week or more for the grieving process to be accomplished. For some persons there may come a period of time after the completion of all ritual memories when more emotions will have to be discharged. I remember one highly complex woman who, after completion of the bulk of her ritual memories, still had a profusion of emotions "locked behind a door." We had several sessions where God would open the door a crack and she would cry and scream and hold onto me for about an hour. Then God would close the door again until our next meeting.

Demons will be attached to SRA memories. The way they are removed varies greatly from person to person. They seem to act out more in those with highly complex DID. Some persons will complete a memory and the demons will just quietly leave as though discharging the memory released their hold on the person. At other times the same person may need to have demons cast out. Demons can manifest in a person at any time during the memory process. With non-SRA memories, demons are more likely to leave with no manifesting. This subject is covered more thoroughly Chapter 11.

Abuse causes persons to believe lies about themselves, life and God. These lies must be recognized and renounced and then replaced with the truth. The lies programmed into the person by the cult will often be so strong she can only receive the truth from Jesus Christ Himself. Those who have suffered

SRA see beyond the veil into the realm of spirit. Therefore, in addition to their ability to see and hear demons, they also have the ability to see and hear Jesus to a certain extent. If this is the survivor's first experience with Christ-centered prayer ministry, she probably doesn't know this. The spiritual director, by faith, must ask Jesus to come and minister to this person. The abused person needs to be encouraged to look for Him. When she experiences the presence of Jesus, Jesus will tell her the truth through words and/or pictures. It is imperative that the person know the truth before the ministry session is terminated. For example, it would be dangerous for someone to leave believing she caused the death of innocent children, etc. Many of these beliefs are designed to make the person feel hopelessly evil and suicidal. The spiritual director must then reinforce the truth Jesus has revealed to the person. It is often helpful for the survivor to verbally renounce the lies and confess the truth. Even though Jesus has shown her the truth, it helps to speak it forth. At this point demons often try to interfere and need to be cast out.

After experiencing an abuse memory, the individual needs to be comforted. This will take time but it is an important part of the healing process and must not be rushed. Part of being comforted is accomplished through replacing the lies with truth. The Lord Himself will bring comfort as He reveals the truth. Also He may do other things such as embrace them, play with the child alters for awhile, give them a little gift, let them hold a baby who died in a ritual but is alive in heaven, etc. (This all takes place in a dimension of the spirit that we don't experience when we've not been so abused. We don't see this but the survivor tells us what is happening.) The spiritual helper needs to spend time letting the person talk about all that has just transpired. At this point the individual should be experiencing a feeling of peace. It is most important for the survivor to know that the spiritual helper still loves and accepts her even after hearing the horrible experience of the memory. No matter how clearly the helper understands that the survivor was an innocent victim, the abused person will often feel responsible for what transpired at the ritual. Even after Jesus explains the truth the person often feels responsible for what happened. Overcoming these feelings takes time and unconditional love from the spiritual helper.

The wounded person needs to agree that, with God's help, she will forgive the perpetrators. This is most difficult but absolutely essential. It helps to remind her that forgiveness is a decision of the will and not a feeling. Unforgiveness does nothing to punish the offenders but it will cause the survivor to suffer the torment of bitterness and separation from God. God makes it clear in His word that if we expect to be forgiven we must forgive those who offend us. Sometimes it is helpful to explain that the perpetrators were like human shells totally taken over by demons. It is all right to hate what they did, but the human instrument needs to be forgiven. God will help expedite this process if the person is willing.

All other aspects of the memory must be absolved. If vows were made, they must be broken. Demons may be attached to vows. Sometimes they will leave as the vow is renounced. At other times the person will be unable to renounce the vow until the demon is removed. Vows seem to be guarded by demons. If magic surgery was performed, these "implants" must be "removed" by the Lord. (Magic surgery is explained in Chapter 9.) Demons also guard the magic surgery "devices" and must be removed.

The alters who experienced the abuse memory need to be settled in a safe place. Jesus always sovereignly handles them. I just ask Him what He wants to do with them. He may integrate them or He may take them to a safe place inside and integrate them later. There have been articles and books written detailing how integration should be conducted by the counselor. I believe this is totally unnecessary...Jesus does it all perfectly.

At this point I would like to describe a typical SRA memory and show how these goals were completed. This memory was from a 53-year-old woman with highly complex DID. Her dissociative ability was phenomenal causing her to be sent as a child every summer from her home in rural America to Germany where she was programmed by the most sophisticated programmers with unlimited resources. It is common for children with exceptionally high dissociative ability to be sent to foreign countries during the summer for programming. I chose this particular memory because it is not as brutal as some memories yet it gives the reader some perception of the depth of pain experienced in SRA. Please be reminded that this memory is only one of hundreds of equally painful experiences suffered by just one individual. Persons this severely wounded require a few years of concentrated ministry and love to overcome such deep rending. I say this to counteract the current popular theory that DID/SRA can be healed in a few months time. This memory was about programming for control.

In this memory she was ten years old sitting in an upstairs bedroom in a mansion in Germany. (I watched as this woman held her arms up against her chest and rocked back and forth.) In the memory she was comforting a blue-eyed, fuzzy-haired little baby the cultists had given her to baby sit. This little girl had been through many rituals and knew what they did with little babies.

She said, "I know what they're going to do with the baby and I have to save him. If I wait until he goes to sleep maybe I can sneak out with him and get him to the village where someone will protect him."

At last the baby was asleep. With her coat on (it was a brisk fall day) she tiptoed down the stairs with the baby in her arms and out the front door. She walked quickly zigzagging as she went in an effort to confuse the dogs she knew would soon be following. Her plan was to cross the river thereby throwing off the dogs' scent and hopefully make it to the village.

She stepped into the water; it was extremely cold but she was determined to save the baby at all cost. Continuing into the ever-deepening water, holding the baby high above her head, she noticed there was no sound of barking dogs. They hadn't noticed she was gone. Maybe she could make it!

Suddenly, with no warning, she heard the click of a rifle bolt as she was simultaneously shoved under the water by a dog that had been swimming silently behind her. She fought desperately to hold the baby above water but the dog was holding her down to the point she was struggling desperately for survival. There was no way she could hold the baby above water.

The next thing she remembered was the men taking her and the dead baby back to the mansion where they repeatedly shamed her for killing the baby. This baby was not chosen for sacrifice, they said. They had only wanted her to baby sit. Now she was a wicked, evil murderer. How could she do such a thing!

She was forced to dry the dead baby and then dress it in burial clothes. They had a tiny ruffled blouse, leggings and booties for the baby. (Imagine the agony of a ten-year-old girl being told she killed a helpless baby and then having to dress it for burial!)

She was instructed to put the baby in a box and then everyone went outside for the burial. The men dug a hole in the ground and had her place the box with the dead baby inside into the hole and throw dirt upon it.

By the end of the memory she was crying over and over, "You can do anything you want to with me. I don't care. I will do whatever you say." In her mind she was a despicable murderer who deserved the greatest punishment available.

They forced her to sign papers with her own blood saying she would forever be loyal to Satan and would willingly obey every cult edict for the rest of her life.

She was then subjected to a ritual that lasted most of the night. The Lord said He didn't want either of us to know what was done to her in that ritual but He did let her know she was bedridden and unable to walk for several days. She had not resisted them in any of their tortures that night.

The horror, guilt, and pain of this memory were horrendous. I tried to reassure her that the whole event had been planned by her perpetrators and that the baby would have been sacrificed anyway. Her unbridled weeping and wailing totally drowned out my voice as I attempted to restrain her from beating her face with her fists. In times such as these the desire to bring an end to their crying is great but the pain must be released. She needed plenty of time to release her emotions without injuring herself.

Demons then began to surface with accusations such as, "She is a murderer and you know it! She loved it when that baby died! She has killed many babies, you know, even her own! Why do you have her in your house? She is evil and vile and deserves to die for what she did." As each demon surfaced I cast him out. There is no need to ask their names...just tell them to shut up and get out in Jesus' name.

After the demons had left and she had expressed enough of her emotions that she was able to calm down, I asked the Lord to minister to her and show her the truth. The Lord showed her that as she was rocking the baby in the upstairs bedroom, the men were gathered in a room downstairs waiting for her to come down the stairs. As one of them watched through a small crack in the door another asked, "Is she there yet?" He answered, "Not yet." And then "Here she comes now." They watched as she left the house. Then they followed quietly from a distance so they would not be detected. They knew at some point they would release the dogs and the baby would be killed. The Lord also showed her that the baby was marked for sacrifice. Had he not died by drowning he would have died in the ritual that night...drowning was more merciful. The Lord said He took the baby immediately. He let her see the baby and hold him. (This is all done in the spiritual dimension that the rest of us do not experience.) She knew the baby was alive and well in a glorious place where there is no suffering. The lies had been replaced by the truth.

One who has not experienced such pain might think the issue was now settled but it just isn't that easy. The emotions continued to rage. The belief that she purposely caused the baby's death had to be continually brought captive to the obedience of Christ (*2 Cor. 10:4-5: For the weapons of our warfare are not carnal, but mighty through God to the pulling down of strong holds; Casting down imaginations, and every high thing that exalteth itself against the knowledge of God, and bringing into captivity every thought to the obedience of Christ.*) Grief has to go through all its stages until acceptance and healing come. A memory this painful may require one or two weeks for processing through the grief.

Next the vows made with the signing of the papers needed to be broken. It was impossible for her to repeat a prayer to break the vows until the demons connected to the vows were removed. They surfaced saying things like, "She signed those papers in her own blood. A blood covenant cannot be broken. She belongs to us." After they were cast out she was able to renounce her vows and state that she belonged to Jesus Christ and chose of her own free will to serve and obey Him. The Lord showed her the papers as He burned them up.

I put my arms around her and comforted her while reassuring her that the baby's death was not her fault. The Lord gathered together all the alters that had been formed during this ordeal and merged them into the presenting person.

I believe this example makes it clear why this kind of memory has to be completely resolved in one session. To have stopped at any stage before the completion of all the goals would have left this person extremely vulnerable to demonic attacks and suicide. This lady needed daily contact from me for several days until this memory's pain was diminished. Please keep in mind this was only one of a multitude of equally or more painful memories in one person. Abuse of this depth requires years of ministry rather than a few months. There should be no attempt for shortcuts with abuse of this magnitude.

CHAPTER SEVEN

VALIDITY OF MEMORIES AND FAMILY ABUSE

In this section I will be combining the subjects of family and validity of memories. If a person's memories of familial abuse are true, then she should have no further contact with family until she is totally healed. In some cases she should never see them again. If her memories are not genuine, then a family is being separated and innocent people are being hurt. Therefore, it is essential to know whether or not the memories are true and then act accordingly.

In families where generational Satanism is practiced, the whole family is involved...mother, father, brothers, sisters, grandparents, aunts, uncles, and cousins. It is difficult for anyone to escape from a family this deeply enmeshed in the occult. It is especially problematic for the perpetrators. I believe they fall into the category described in I Timothy 4:1,2: *Now the Spirit speaketh expressly, that in the latter times some shall depart from the faith, giving heed to seducing spirits, and doctrines of devils; speaking lies in hypocrisy; having their conscience seared with a hot iron.* When one hears what these people do, it appears that they have no conscience. Without a conscience it is impossible to respond to God's love and the conviction of the Holy Spirit. They are driven by demons to commit more and more crimes to attain the same level of excitement and power. The other difficulty with a perpetrator escaping is that the cult typically hunts them down for the purpose of torturing them to death. They've all seen it done to defectors and believe there is no way out.

The victims sometimes escape because somewhere deep in their heart they never acquiesced to Satan. They hated the violence and evil and cried out for God to save them; therefore, their conscience remained sensitive. They are able to love God and seek Him. God desires to guide them to someone who will help them. They don't remember the way defectors were tortured because they may not remember being in a cult in the first place. Once they begin remembering they will be able to understand that God is supernaturally protecting them as long as they are obedient to God and stay under godly authority. (See Chapter 4, The Principle of Authority.)

It is extremely difficult for many SRA persons to believe their family could have done to them the things to which their memories attest. This is most confusing. They look at their family of origin (who are still living or who, perhaps, are only in the conscious memory) and then at their abuse memories and the dichotomy is so great it seems unbelievable. This can result in tremendous confusion and extreme feelings of guilt. They may feel that they are evil to "make up" these terrible stories about their family, and that God is angry with them for saying anything against father or mother.

When God is leading the spiritual helper, the repressed memories will be released only by the unction of the Holy Spirit, quite unlike the hypnosis commonly used in secular counseling. The supernatural nature of this approach helps reduce the potential for false memories. Many times during the course of a memory God will allow things to occur that will validate the truthfulness of the memory.

The veracity of the memory may be validated by "body memory." As the survivor is relating to you what was done (or as she actually relives the whole experience in front of you as though she were just now experiencing it [abreaction]), marks correlating exactly to the memory may appear on her body.

I remember a time when a woman was telling me about being ritually abused in one of Hitler's death camps many years after WWII had ended. (Unbelievable as it may seem, for many years the Satanists have been flying their victims to Germany to put them through terrible rituals in those camps to put the spirits of the Holocaust into their victims to bring back to the United States to be released here.) As this woman was telling me about being hung by her hair and branded on her face, I was wondering if this really happened. To my total amazement a cross appeared on her cheek and remained there for just a few minutes and then faded away. The cross appeared to be about 2 ½ inches tall and was white with the skin surrounding it being a dark pink. There was no doubt about what I saw. I no longer distrusted this woman's account.

A similar incident occurred with the woman whose husband claimed she was not SRA. (An account of his accusations against me and the resultant disruption in our church is told in detail in the chapter entitled *The Exchanged Life.*) She was abreacting a memory of being held over a fire during a ritual. I saw her skin turn a blotchy beet red and perspiration roll down her face during the memory. I thank God He showed me this so that when accusations came and the professionals said I was wrong, I could recall this and other manifestations and know without a doubt I was not mistaken. At the time of the allegations, I of course said nothing about this to anyone as I had to maintain confidentiality that resulted in my not being able to defend myself.

Body memory may also take the form of physical actions that correspond to the memory. For example, it is not uncommon for SRA persons to have memories of having been severely shocked with electric current. Their body will often go through the jerking motions of the shock as the memory is relived. At this point a demon will usually exit. Electric shock seems to be a way of putting demons into a person. When these demons leave, the body often goes through the same jerking motions that were experienced at the time of the shock.

I remember one interesting type of body memory exhibited by a six-year-old alter manifesting in a fifty-year-old woman. She commented that she had just lost her two front teeth. As she recounted her ordeal she continually put her tongue in the "space" where the two teeth "had been" and lisped as she talked.

Another way God may validate a memory is through the manifestation of demons. As a survivor is telling what happened a demon may surface and say things like, "This never happened to her! She is just making this up! Don't believe her! She is insane! Don't listen to her!" The more we are able to let God be in charge of the ministry, the more perfectly He will control the demons and the alters. God is able, when we give Him control, to keep the demons locked up until it is time for them to be removed or until God wants to use them for a purpose such as validating a memory. He will also keep alters hidden away until it is time for them to surface.

The extreme emotional impact of a memory also attests to its veracity. During the course of a memory persons may sob uncontrollably, scream, hyperventilate, or even experience gagging or dry heaves. In an attempt to lessen their emotional pain they may beat on themselves or bite their arm. It is quite common for them to physically recoil in their chair in an attempt to distance themselves as much as possible from their spiritual helper because they feel they are too evil or vile to be near anyone. Sometimes they attempt to leave the room to escape their pain. This kind of behavior attests to the fact that these are not fabricated stories from someone's vivid imagination.

As SRA memories are relived, a spiritual helper will often observe the person switching from alter to alter as the account is verbalized. Most rituals are too horrendous for one alter to handle. It is not uncommon for three, four or more alters to surface one at a time in order to complete one entire ritual memory. The last alter may say he/she felt nothing or he/she enjoyed the whole episode and that the other alters are "sniveling little wimps." It would take a top-notch Hollywood performer to fake this kind of presentation.

A memory may be validated by another person having a similar memory. A man described to me a recurring dream in which he found himself required to dive down a hole in the ground that passed through the very center of the earth. On the other side he met and talked with some men about something dreadfully important which he couldn't remember. Then he had to go back into the hole and as he passed through the center of the earth, the hole (or tube) in which he was traveling intersected another. Just as he passed through the center, another person or being passed through the center also so that their beings passed through each other. When I heard this account, I recognized it to be a type of so-called "spirit travel." The fact that it was recurring, seemed incredibly real and was very upsetting to him indicated to me that this was not just a dream. It was a demonic spiritual experience that can occur as a result of cult abuse. He felt alone in his experience and wanted to know if anyone I knew had ever had such an incident.

The next day a close SRA friend and confidant who desires to help others by sharing some of her experiences had a memory of passing through a tunnel through the very center of the earth. She found herself in Germany listening to some people relating something to her of great importance. She then passed back through the center of the earth and in the process passed through another being. The amazing thing is, she knew nothing about this man's experience!

(I need to add at this point that in no way do I believe a human spirit leaves the body and travels around. The Bible tells us, "For as the body without the spirit is dead, so faith without works is dead also" [James 2:26]. "Spirit travel" is demonic trickery, but this depth of deception is only possible when a person has been involved in occult practices. Demons can make a person believe that in the spirit they are interacting with other persons, traveling to other places and even make them feel tired when they get back. However, the only time the spirit leaves the body is at death, and it is appointed unto men once to die [Heb. 9:27].)

When she started into this memory I grabbed my tape recorder (with her permission) believing God had brought this memory at this time to help my other friend understand he was not alone in his experience. This was certainly no coincidence. (I had her permission years ago to tape record anything I deemed necessary. She has allowed some of her tapes to be shared for educational purposes.) This whole account was related by a very young child alter who talked baby talk and likened her experience to Alice falling down a rabbit hole in *Alice in Wonderland*. This amplified the validity of her account. This is the only time I have shared a tape of one SRA person's experience with another and it was only done by permission with prayer and God's specific guidance. The tape was not emotional nor was there any expression of pain that would be upsetting to another person.

To maintain the authenticity of the memories, it is most important that the spiritual director never ask leading questions. A leading question would be something like, "Did they wear black robes?" or "Did they kill the baby?" That is interjecting something into the memory that the person might not remember but with the suggestion might incorporate into the memory. Better questions would be, "What happened next?" or "What were you feeling?"

When memories of familial abuse begin surfacing it is essential for the person to break all communication with family members for a period of time. In the most severe cases she should never see or communicate with family ever again. When there is SRA, there is deep programming that gives perpetrators tremendous control over the survivor. Curses, demons, voodoo, etc. will be directed almost nonstop against the survivor. She also may be programmed to commit suicide should she ever begin divulging memories. If we have committed our ministry into God's hands, He will protect her from her self-destructive programming.

It is common for the survivor to want contact with family members even though she knows they abused her horribly. The programming to return to the family can be incredibly powerful. Along with the programming is the desire to make things right. She may feel that if she could express her forgiveness to them and discuss the past with them, they might be reasonable and family relationships could begin again on a new foundation. This is totally out of the question. People who do these things are not reasonable. There can be no reconciliation short of a miracle from God, this kind of miracle being unlikely because God will not usurp someone's will and perpetrators have turned their will over to the Devil. In cases where abuse was slight there may be the possibility of seeing family members after memories are completed and healing has come; however, the survivor should never be alone with them. When it is generational SRA and the whole family is involved, there is usually no chance of reconciliation.

When I say there is no chance of reconciliation, some may think I'm being too extreme. Those who would say this haven't heard the memories. The people who do these things to other human beings, to say nothing of children and their own family members, are barely human themselves. They are so overtaken by demons that there is very little of the actual person left. They are more like human shells totally possessed by demons. You can't reason with a demon. There is not the slightest touch of compassion or decency in a demon or in the persons who willingly give themselves over to them.

There may be someone within the family who is also a victim rather than a perpetrator who would genuinely want a relationship with the survivor. This would not be possible until the person is totally healed and then contact would have to be monitored. This is because the family member who has not gotten free is still enmeshed in and controlled by the family. He/she would be used, even against his/her will, to bring harm to the survivor.

The people who subject their children to SRA are wicked beyond belief. One reason this kind of abuse is allowed to continue is that most people won't believe this degree of depravity and wickedness exists in the communities and towns of our nation...but it does! The humanistic lie that human beings are basically good has so permeated our culture that the truth of Jeremiah 17:9, *The heart is deceitful above all things, and desperately wicked: who can know it?* has been cast aside.

Someone escaping from a family enmeshed in generational Satanism typically will have memories of many murders and other gruesome and unlawful activities. If these atrocities could be proven in court (which they can't), the perpetrators would be convicted of crimes deserving the death penalty. The severely ritually abused person will have much detailed information stored in the deep recesses of her mind that the cult does not want revealed. For this reason her life would be in danger from family members and other cult persons should she speak publicly about her abuse. I want to add that there might be a situation where God would lead someone to prosecute, especially if children are being abused like in a daycare for example, but generally it is best not to attempt any legal justice. As with everything else in SRA ministry, we are better off entrusting everything into God's hands.

It is fruitless to try to prove these crimes in our courts for the following reasons:

1. A jury won't believe that people in their community are capable of such heinous acts.
2. A jury will require evidence that cannot be produced.
3. The survivor's cult family may be well-respected members of the community.
4. The judge, lawyers or a jurist may be members of a satanic cult.
5. The memories cannot be proven. Often the incidents remembered occurred decades ago.
6. The average person, having no knowledge of how the mind works, probably will not believe that dissociated memories can be valid.
7. Any court action would place your survivor friend in a situation of incredible suffering, community exposure and possible ridicule. She might well be slapped with a label of some kind of mental illness and locked into an identity box by her peers from which she might never escape.
8. The media would create negative public response to the trial.
9. The cults really do have tremendous power over the minds of individuals who have not yielded their heart to Jesus Christ. Cults would network to send forth powerful demons to blind the minds of the trial participants.

When abused persons have separated from their family of origin, they need new relationships to replace the old. This is where the church can minister the healing love of Christ into these lives. It is not advisable to openly make known the fact that someone has been ritually abused. Church people willing to reach out to lonely abused persons may turn away in fear at the mention of satanic cults. In reality they have nothing to fear, but many Christians have not yet comprehended the protection, power and authority they have in Jesus Christ.

There are some kinds of memories we have not yet discussed. Sometimes a spiritual director may hear accounts of bizarre events that are obviously impossible and yet the survivor is greatly distressed over them. Their anguish seems genuine but the memory is impossible. An example of this would be a "memory" of having the parts of their body severed and then reassembled. This would fall into the category of "magic surgery." The individual was probably hypnotized and/or given drugs and subjected to a contrived experience to invoke extreme trauma and display the "powers" of Satan. The survivor needs our love and comfort during her memory. When the memory has been completed and the pain released, she needs to be told the truth...that the cult contrived the experience and Satan does not have these powers.

Because the ritually abused are open to the demonic realm, they will have dreams of a spiritual nature that are so real they cannot discern if it actually happened or if it was a dream. Demons take advantage of this and will use dreams to attempt to destroy the survivor's trust in her spiritual helper. Survivors may have dreams of the spiritual helper abandoning them, humiliating them, giving them over to the cult, etc. Even though we pray against this phenomenon, there doesn't seem to be a way of effectively preventing it. We need to be aware that this kind of dream may cause a survivor to seem inexplicably cold and distant or try to alienate herself from her spiritual director. If the spiritual director senses this distancing occurring, it is often advisable to ask the survivor if she has had this type of dream.

CHAPTER EIGHT

IDENTIFYING DID/SRA

The Spirit of the Lord is upon me, because he hath anointed me to preach the gospel to the poor; he hath sent me to heal the brokenhearted, to preach deliverance to the captives, and recovering of sight to the blind, to set at liberty them that are bruised, to preach the acceptable year of the Lord. (Luke 4:18,19).

These are the words of Jesus in Luke as He stood before the congregation in the synagogue at the beginning of his ministry. Then He added, *This day is this scripture fulfilled in your ears.* Truly Jesus did all of the things mentioned in this passage and more, not only for His generation, but also for all who would believe in Him in every generation. The same Spirit that was upon Jesus is upon those of us who believe in Him! We are called to the same good works.

Those who have been satanically ritually abused suffer with hearts so broken they are shattered. Many, as little children, were never allowed to form an authentic identity but through abuse were shattered into many personality fragments. Such individuals long to find their own identity, but the pain of their "bruising" is so severe, they are hopelessly locked away in dungeons within themselves—dark places of despair with no hope of ever being delivered.

In a society that is ignorant of SRA or refuses to believe in its existence, where can such persons find help? Very little, if anything, is taught about SRA in our universities; therefore, most mental health professionals are not quick to recognize the signs of SRA and identify its existence.

The startling truth is that most persons who were satanically ritually abused have no memory of their abuse. They may suffer various mental and emotional problems but have absolutely no conscious memory of their abuse. How can this be? The answer to this question is both psychological and spiritual.

The trauma of SRA is so extremely severe that the memory of even one episode could cause a person to suffer a complete mental breakdown. And yet, some people have experienced literally hundreds of terrifying rituals. They are able to survive the shock of such horror by dissociating. That is to say, they experience a split in the conscious process in which a group of mental activities breaks away from the main stream of consciousness and functions as a separate unit, as if belonging to another person. By dissociating they are able to believe their experience happened to someone else; they erect a wall of amnesia and are totally unaware that anything happened. The ability to do this varies with individuals, but the fact is, many persons can completely "forget" what happened for decades— perhaps their entire lifetime.

The fact that they don't remember the abuse doesn't keep them from suffering from its effects. Satanically ritually abused persons often suffer from various forms of mental illness as well as many physical problems. When someone receives help from mental health professionals for a period of years without overcoming his/her neuroses, he/she may be suffering the effects of SRA.

I believe that God, in His infinite mercy, often helps them keep their memories suppressed until He can connect them with a Christian helper prepared by the Holy Spirit to effectively minister for SRA. Effective ministry may begin with being alert to the fact that satanic ritual abuse and its resultant DID (it is probably impossible to survive SRA without dissociating) is not at all uncommon. If one is not looking for it, one probably will not recognize it.

Some persons who have been satanically ritually abused have never sought counseling or professional help of any kind. Their life appears normal on the surface and they remember nothing about their abuse, but they are never free to be truly happy. One example comes to mind.

Carl, a man in his sixties, is a sincere Christian man who has whole-heartedly pursued a relationship with Jesus Christ for many decades. My husband and I have known him for many years. He is basically healthy, has a happy marriage, a nice home, good church relationships and seemingly everything he could need to be happy. However, Carl has never been able to overcome his feelings that he would "just rather go be with Jesus." He often feels that he wants to leave everything and go live in a cabin in the mountains of Montana. His faithful pursuit of God has brought many victories in his life but deep down he has never felt happy or fulfilled in life.

Noticing that there was no current reason for Carl to feel this way, my husband and I began to suspect that he was experiencing emotions connected to some serious childhood abuse issues that needed ministry. Carl was very open to talking with us about his feelings. I began to write down every indicator of abuse we discerned. Writing things down or making a list helps us get below the surface of what appears to be a normal life and discern whether or not there has been abuse. When many indicators are present, even though there are no abuse memories, it is extremely likely that the person was seriously abused.

The first thing we noticed about Carl was that he had dissociated. He had absolutely no memories of his childhood before the age of six. Other entire years of his life seemed to be missing as he had no recollection of them. His wife indicated what we had also observed, that one never knew what "mood" Carl would be in. There were times when he appeared happy and his wonderful sense of humor would have us all laughing. But more often than not, Carl would be quiet, speaking only when spoken to, and just sitting in front of his computer playing computer games for hours on end. It was obvious that he had built up many walls to hide behind that no one could penetrate. His wife told us that Carl sometimes had no memory of things they had done together just days earlier. It soon became evident that Carl had different alters that were out at different times. He was not moody...he was dissociated. He could switch in an instant from happy and communicative to silent and reserved.

Carl had been an officer in the United States Marine Corps. He had a big gun collection and loved to shoot, but at the same time, he liked stuffed animals, an indication that he had some child alters.

There were many signs of abuse in his life. Carl was good at acting like he had no problems, but actually he had suffered from depression all his life. He just didn't talk about it. He hated himself and felt he was somehow defective and inferior to others. He felt that he had been destined for failure in life...that he could never succeed no matter how hard he tried. This left him feeling hopeless with the anticipation that he would always fail in everything he attempted. Others could see that he was a gifted, intelligent person who had helped many people and that the world was a much better place because he was in it, but there was no way to make him see this about himself.

People close to Carl sensed that he was angry. He controlled his anger well, but it erupted from time to time in frustration over little things in life. When we talked with him about anger, he admitted that it was like a deep pit inside him that was constantly seething. He had just learned to keep the lid on it. When children are mistreated, they get angry and will remain angry until they receive ministry for their abuse.

Carl was able to remember cutting himself when he was an adolescent. He took a sharp knife and started beating the palm of his hand with the blade until his hand was all bloody. He had to be careful to conceal it from his parents until it was healed. He doesn't remember why he did it, but he must have felt extreme emotional distress to do such a thing. Cutting was another item to add to our list.

A tendency towards addictions had been with him all his life—cigarettes, alcohol, food and computer games headed the list. He had overcome most of these with God's help but he still needed sweets and snacks as comfort foods.

Carl's family attended church faithfully, but it was the kind of church you could attend for years without ever hearing the Gospel message. One time he and his mother attended a service in a different church where Carl heard the Gospel presented in a way he could understand. When the invitation was made for people to come down front, Carl rose to go down, but his mother held him back. God saw his heart though and Carl was drawn to his Heavenly Father and began seeking a relationship. He read the Bible every night all the years of his youth. Years later he accepted the call into fulltime pastoral ministry.

One can't help wondering why his mother held him back. Was she in a hurry to leave because it was late? Did it make her feel that she had not done a good job of raising her son in the church? Would she experience the wrath of her husband if she allowed her son to go down front and he found out about it? We will never know, but it is just another memory for Carl that fit into the pattern of always being held back from the things he wanted to do.

As we talked further with Carl we began to see overwhelming evidence of satanic ritual abuse in his life. We had known a lot of these facts about him, but until these indicators were listed on paper, we had no idea there were so many. If there had been only a few, we would not have suspected SRA, but in Carl's case, the list was very long. The evidence was indisputable. Here are some of the evidences of SRA we found.

Carl was dismayed that his parents never showed him any affection. He was not kissed, hugged, patted on the back or in any way shown affection. The only time his father spoke to him was to correct him in a harsh tone of voice that registered to Carl as disgust and distain. As an adult looking back he felt that his mother loved him but was not able to express herself in an affectionate way. This was a strong indicator of SRA because in Satanism, the chosen child is not to be shown affection. The mother often wants to express demonstrable love to the child but is forbidden to by the father.

Carl lamented that part of him felt dead inside. He had been faithful in prayer, Bible study and his pursuit of God. He knew he had a relationship with Jesus Christ, but somehow this dead part never came alive. This was an indication that dissociated parts were locked away inside in inaccessible places such as dungeons, mazes, boxes, etc. (More of this is explained in Chapter Nine.)

Carl was raised with the impression that he was not very bright intellectually. In adulthood he took a battery of tests related to his work that indicated he had a very high IQ and should have been a scientist or medical doctor. This made him feel that he had been ripped off, held back and not allowed to succeed. SRA children are usually very bright but are programmed to believe they are stupid. Success often eludes their grasp.

Carl was accident prone—a strong indicator of curses on his life. Anyone who knew him was aware that he often had gashes on his head from running into things. His wife said she could not count all the times she had helped stop the bleeding on his head after he rammed it into the corner of a shelf, the trunk of the car, a kitchen cabinet door, etc. There had been numerous woodcutting accidents, including a chain saw cut to his knee and a missing fingertip from an axe mishap.

But with all the stubbed toes and other painful episodes, there was a certain grace of God upon his life. God's hand was upon him. God had ministry plans for his life and the enemy was only allowed to go so far but no further. This tendency for accidents is a common indication of SRA. Some SRA persons, rather than having accidents, have numerous sicknesses—or they may be plagued with both!

Carl had an unexplained fear of heights. He had no re-membrance of why this would be, but he never went near the window when in a tall building. This, too, is a common indica-tor of SRA. Children are often dangled off the edge of a high cliff or bridge and threatened in some way in order to gain control over them and make them dissociate.

The strongest indicator of SRA was found in the fact that his father and one of his grandfathers had been 32nd degree Masons. Carl's first and middle name were his grandfather's name. His grandfather had been the "Worshipful Master" of the lodge in his hometown. It is well known that high degree Mason's are into Satanism.

His grandfather was also German. There is a lot of Satan-ism in families with Germanic heritage.

With all the above indicators plus others not mentioned here, it was certain in our minds that Carl was satanically ritually abused. After much prayer, we decided to tell him our findings. Sometimes we wait until the person has a memory, but the Lord indicated we were to tell him what we had dis-covered.

As Carl thought about this, it seemed incredulous, but he could see that the evidence was strong. We continued to pray for him and it was not long until he had a memory and other things happened that left no doubt about the nature of his abuse. From the progress he is making (this has just happened) we can see that he is well on his way to finally overcoming and experiencing the joy Jesus Christ has for him.

The following is a concise list of all the indicators of abuse, dissociation and SRA we noticed about Carl:

Deprived of touch and affection
Made to feel stupid
Father showed only distain
No guidance for anything in life from his father
Cutting self
Not allowed to go forward for altar call
Accident prone
Risk taking (evidence of desire to die)
Lifetime depression
Desire to not exist
Desire to flee
Self-hatred
Observed dissociation
Inability to overcome after a lifetime of seeking God
Feeling he has been ripped off by life
Some affinity for stuffed animals (child alters)
Feelings of failure
Fear of heights
Expectation to be rejected
Open to curses
Internal rage
Part of him feels dead
No memories before age six
Other years of memories missing

Deep-seated feelings of shame
Father and grandfather 32nd degree Masons
Feels need to have TV or radio on when alone
Uncomfortable if anything in room is out of place
German ancestry
Chronic acid stomach
Knee problems
Some arthritis
Blood chemistry imbalance
Nightmares resembling abuse rituals
Tendency for addictions
Dreams of helping internal children

Evidences of Dissociation

At this point I will list some of the indications of dissociation which can occur with or without SRA. Dissociation is often the result of SRA but there are instances where dissociation occurs from childhood abuse other than satanic rituals.

The Old Testament Hebrew word for evil is *ra'* from the root word *ra'a'*, meaning to spoil by breaking to pieces. This is what happens when little children are subjected to unbearable evil. Inside they break into pieces and are cut off from themselves. Dissociation is a split in the conscious process. During intolerable suffering a group of mental activities breaks away from the main stream of consciousness and functions as a separate unit, as though belonging to a separate person. This is how "multiple personalities" or "dissociative identities" are formed.

1. Memory loss - Persons who have used dissociation as their main coping mechanism may be unable to remember some of the common experiences from childhood. They may complain that their past seems to be "full of holes." They may comment that

years seem to have disappeared from their past. This leaves them with the feeling they are somehow less than whole persons.

2. Time loss - Some persons experience the phenomenon of losing hours out of a day. They may realize it is four o'clock in the afternoon but their last memory was of eating breakfast. They may find themselves in a strange location with no memory of how they got there.

3. Hearing voices - They may have conversations with another voice in their head or hear others talking inside their head. Voices may be demons or they may be alters formed through dissociation.

4. History of headaches - The process of "switching" to another personality often causes headaches. Persons who switch several times a day may feel they have a perpetual headache. During ministry, a severe headache often precedes a memory.

5. Changes in handwriting - If the spiritual helper is suspecting DID/MPD (dissociative identity disorder, formerly called multiple personality disorder) it might be advisable to ask the survivor to keep a daily journal where feelings, events of the day, scriptural insights and dreams are hand scribed. Distinct changes in handwriting may be noticed if DID/MPD is present.

6. Observed dissociation during ministry - The discerning spiritual friend may notice changes of "personalities" during the course of conversation. For example the person may suddenly change from being distressed to being calm. Sometimes a slight shaking of the head or fluttering of the eyelids will be noticed.

7. Cognizance of internal children or personalities - The person may be aware of little children inside, perhaps many, or other personalities.

8. Frequent changing of clothing - Some persons change clothing several times a day because different alters want to wear outfits complementing their distinct personalities. A male alter will insist on wearing slacks or jeans, a seductive alter may desire low-cut blouses, etc. Also frequently rearranging furniture follows the same principle—different alters have their opinion about how the room should look.

9. Very few clothing ensembles - Some persons may tire of the endless bickering over clothing by their alters and strip their wardrobe to only a few items.

10. A sense of deprivation - Some people with DID/MPD feel they have missed out on life. This may stem from not being able to remember much of it. For example one woman felt deep regret over the fact that she could remember very little of her relationship with her son as he was growing up. She felt she had missed the experience of parenting because most of it was forgotten.

11. Inordinate desire to please others - An abused child learns to try to please everyone in hopes of not being severely punished.

12. Intelligent and creative - These characteristics are necessary to have the ability to dissociate. Creativity may be evidenced in poetry, art, music, etc.

13. A highly developed imagination - When abuse is severe and there is no safe place for escape, a child has to go inward into the imagination and invent his/her own safe world.

14. A desire to play with or collect stuffed animals - Because the person may never have been allowed to be a child, child alters may surface when alone and want to play.

15. Emotions disconnected from cognitive thoughts - The ability to talk about horrendous abuse (which

has not been healed) with no emotion may be an indication that one personality is describing something that happened to another personality.

The ability to dissociate is a marvelous coping mechanism that enables one to experience episodes of horror that would otherwise drive one insane. The mental health community has changed the term "multiple personality disorders" to "dissociative identity disorders" in recent years.

I believe this term is far better and less confusing than "multiple personality disorder." Some persons upon learning they were MPD felt they were "crazy" or "hopelessly insane." This is not the case but labels are sometimes frightening and confining. The words multiple personalities may have caused some persons to think they had more than one soul and spirit...that there were other human entities living within them. Then there were those who became enamored with their "fascinating" condition (Hollywood movies such as *Sybil* or *The Three Faces of Eve* may have glamorized MPD to the public) and they began to base an identity around it.

Some abused persons who have developed the coping mechanism of dissociation have never learned any other means of coping. If they are particularly gifted in this area, they will continue to dissociate whenever life seems unbearable. During ministry, this method of coping needs to be discouraged and new coping mechanisms taught and encouraged.

When a Christian chooses to "split" rather than cope using God's help, the alter formed through this splitting will be an unbeliever because it was formed in unbelief. This alter, being an unbeliever, becomes a pawn in the control of demons who will use the alter to work against the survivor to harm her. When the spiritual friend discerns this has occurred, he/she needs to either lead the alter to a commitment to Christ or ask God to put the alter away in a safe place until a future time when he/she can be dealt with. I often pray and lock them up over the telephone. Sometimes when I'm not available God sovereignly locks them up and then releases them during our ministry time.

When a survivor submits under the authority of a godly spiritual friend and prayer is paramount in the ministry process, the Sovereign Lord does awesome and mighty deeds to protect His wounded little lambs. An example of this just occurred. As I was writing this passage I received a phone call from one of my survivor friends from her office. Her pager had vibrated indicating she was getting an incoming call from me. She called to ask why I had just called her. The amazing thing is, I hadn't called her, but my number appeared on her pager! As we talked the Lord prompted a cult alter (an alter formed and programmed by the cult years ago to sabotage the survivor should she begin disclosing memories) to speak and boast that she was going to call my friend's brother (one of her main perpetrators who would bring her great harm). I had the opportunity to pray and the Lord put the alter away until I could work with her later.

Indications of SRA

The following are some of the symptoms that may be evidenced in a survivor of satanic ritual abuse. Several of these indicators should be observed before SRA is considered. Characteristics of DID should also be present.

1. Fear of crowds - Rituals are often held in crowded rooms or there may be outdoor rituals attended by large numbers of people. One SRA woman was terrified at a Fourth of July outdoor celebration where a large number of people were gathered after dark in a field. It reminded her of an outdoor ritual gathering.
2. Fear of water - A common means of control is to hold the subject's head under water.
3. Dislike or fear of dogs - Bestiality is often forced upon SRA children and women.

4. Inordinate fear of snakes or spiders - A child may have been restrained while snakes or spiders were allowed to crawl on him/her.

5. Inordinate fear of bees - A survivor may have been subjected to multiple bee stings.

6. Fear of drugs - The SRA person may have been drugged while being forced to do things against his/her will. Drugs are also used to open the spirit realm further to increase the torment of their victim.

7. Fear of doctors and hospitals - The survivor may have been subjected to painful medical procedures for evil purposes. Cults often have their own doctors and even clinics (clinics are usually depicted as being in foreign countries.)

8. Fear of prayer - There may be a fear of others gathering around her for prayer. It can remind her of a ritual where she may have been surrounded while people chanted. The spiritual director should ask permission before praying with a new survivor friend and be cautious about "laying on of hands" during prayer.

9. Frequent hand washing, hot showers - Sometimes this is an attempt to wash the blood off one's hands or cleanse the body from shame and guilt. Others cannot see the blood but sometimes a survivor does.

10. Ability to see and hear demons—SRA opens a person's perceptions to the realm of evil spirits that others do not see or hear.

11. Gender confusion - Cults may purposely program confusion regarding gender. For example a woman may dress in a masculine or asexual fashion.

12. Self-mutilation - Cutting, scratching, burning - Persons abused by satanic cults may have been taught to cut themselves as a means of coping with stress.

13. Inability to pray - The SRA survivor may have been programmed for an inability to pray.

14. Inability to read the Bible - The SRA survivor may have been programmed against Bible reading.

15. Fear of God and Jesus - The SRA survivor may have endured painful rituals intended to create a fear of God and Jesus. It is not uncommon for a cult member disguised as Jesus to horribly abuse the person.

16. Memories of numerous rapes - When a woman begins remembering many rapes it is an indication that she may be SRA. Demon powers are stored in a female through rituals. These powers are accessed by perpetrators through rape.

17. Confusion - Cults often program their victims for extreme confusion. They may experience difficulties with reasoning and common sense.

18. Backwards thinking - In cult families children are taught that good is evil and evil is good in every conceivable aspect of life; therefore, their thinking on many issues may seem strange.

19. Nightmares - The survivor may be troubled by dreams with violent or satanic themes.

20. Demons manifesting - Through satanic rituals demons are given control over a person's mind, body and voice. It has been my experience that the most severely abused seem to be the most defenseless against demonic manifestations.

21. Self-punishing - The SRA survivors may have been taught that they must punish themselves for laughing, receiving praise, making a mistake, etc. It is not uncommon for them to hit themselves.

22. Abuse identity - The person seems to be consistently in hurtful situations stemming from a belief that it is his/her role in life to be abused. Others sense their expectation for abuse and act accordingly.

23. Accident prone - Due to demonic influences and curses

placed on the lives of the SRA survivors, some of them seem to experience more than their share of painful accidents.

24. Emotional problems - Low self esteem, guilt, depression, anger, suicidal thoughts, unworthiness, self-hatred, and panic attacks are some of the emotional problems that may plague the SRA survivor.

25. Nighttime demon visitations - The SRA survivor may experience terrifying demon visitations and demon rape at night. The incubus demon sexually attacks women and the succubus sexually attacks men.

26. Inability to wear restrictive clothing - bras, coats

27. Dislike of being touched

28. Inability to tolerate certain sounds - Sounds such as crying babies or children, screaming, dogs licking, lips smacking, etc. may trigger emotions or partial memories of rituals.

29. Troubled by strobe lights or blinking lights - Strobe lights are often used in programming and may induce a trance-like state or fear.

Physical Problems

A person who has suffered SRA may experience several of the following physical problems:

1. Migraine headaches
2. Eating disorders - anorexia, bulimia, obesity, food addictions
3. Sexual dysfunction - aversion to sex or overactive sexually
4. Fibromyalgia
5. Digestive tract problems - acid reflux, ulcers, colitis
6. Blood chemistry imbalance

7. Pain in joints of hips
8. Heart problems
9. History of substance abuse - alcohol, drugs
10. Temporomandibular joint syndrome (TMJ)
11. Hysterectomy
12. Unexplained, intermittent pain in stomach, lower back, vagina, rectum
13. Bowel problems often starting in childhood
14. Unexplained scars or tattoos
15. Liver or adrenal malfunctions, thyroid disorder
16. Diagnosed epileptic
17. Urinary tract infections
18. Collapsed rectal wall
19. Arthritis or lupus
20. Problems with knees
21. Hypertension
22. Choking sensations
23. Missing digits
24. Unidentifiable bruises, cuts, scrapes, etc.

Hopefully this information will help those who feel called to this ministry begin to discern those who may have been satanically ritually abused. Someone exhibiting just a few of the aforementioned characteristics should not be considered SRA, but when there are many indications from at least two categories, one should begin to seriously suspect SRA. Once this is discerned, we can pray for the Holy Spirit to begin revealing past experiences that need to be remembered or we can direct the person to someone else who can effectively minister for SRA.

CHAPTER NINE

MAGIC SURGERY AND THE
STRUCTURE OF THE INNER WORLD

In this chapter we will be addressing what we can expect to encounter in a person who has been satanically ritually abused to a state of high complexity. These individuals will most likely have been born into a family practicing Satanism for generations with abuse beginning in the womb. Not all SRA persons will have the structures and complexity we will be discussing here; however, we should expect to find these things in highly complex multiples and these individuals are not at all rare. Persons called to minister in SRA will encounter these individuals and will need a working knowledge of the things discussed in this chapter. Most persons with this level of complexity will be women; therefore, I will use the feminine gender throughout this chapter.

Satanic ritual abuse and the resulting formation of multiple personalities create an inner state of incredible complexity. The following concepts will seem bizarre or surreal to those of us who are learning about this for the first time; however, we must remember the extraordinary concepts outlined in this chapter represent these persons' only perception of life and reality. Everything they say must be treated with respect and with serious concern no matter how illusory it may seem to us.

As stated previously, the Old Testament Hebrew word for evil is *ra'* from the root word *ra'a* meaning to spoil by breaking into pieces. Through many torturous rituals the soul is split into numerous parts that we call alters (alternate personalities.) Demons are summoned and placed inside to keep the parts separated and alone, inaccessible to the victim. Negative emotions and specific cult jobs are assigned to each alter. These alters work against the individual and for the cult keeping her totally under the cult's control. This becomes a living death...a living hell.

The individual is forced by means of ceaseless abuse and demonic programming to form an inner world of darkness. The Hebrew word for darkness is *cho-shek'* meaning figuratively misery, destruction, death, ignorance, sorrow and wickedness. The cultists' aim is to imprison their victim in a web of misery, destruction and living death from which there is no escape. The person's soul is shattered and each piece enmeshed in a maze of dungeons, prisons, booby traps, demons, etc. in their inner world.

The Inner World

The ritually abused are extremely wounded, broken and confused. Most of them don't understand what has happened to them. All they know is they are hurting and need help. Our only understanding about what the cult does and why, we learn from these dear, hurting, confused people. It is difficult to piece together an accurate picture of their inner world, how it functions, and why it was created in the first place. By combining what I've heard and seen from the ritually abused with my knowledge of Scripture, I have formed my own theory to explain the dynamics with which we are dealing.

We know from Scripture that we have a spirit, a soul and a body. (*1 Thes. 5:23 And the very God of peace sanctify you wholly; and I pray God your whole spirit and soul and body be preserved blameless unto the coming of our Lord Jesus Christ.*) In Genesis 2:7 we are shown how we were created in our three parts. *And the Lord God formed man of the dust of the ground, and breathed into his nostrils the breath of life; and man became a living soul.* The breath of God became man's spirit. When the breath of God came into contact with man's body, a soul was formed. These three components are joined within us.

In Hebrews 4:12 we read that Jesus (Himself being the Word of God) does at some point separate the soul from the spirit. *For the word of God is quick, and powerful, and sharper than any twoedged sword, piercing even to the dividing asunder of soul and spirit, and of the joints and marrow, and is a discerner of the thoughts and intents of the heart.* I believe that as long as our spirit is joined to our soul and body, we are not able to see into the spiritual realm. This is as God intended us to be since Satan and demons could appear as "angels of light" and deceive us. God wants us to be innocent concerning evil. Romans 16:19b says, *I would have you wise unto that which is good, and simple concerning evil.*

This concept of separation of soul and spirit is difficult to explain because there is a separation of soul and spirit that is done by Jesus that is good. As we mature in our Christian faith and die to our selfish motives, we become aware of a separation of soul and spirit. This means that our good works that originate from our spirit are not tied to the carnal motives of our soul. This separation is not total because there is still a connection that keeps our spirit contained within our body. We do become more aware of the Holy Spirit and we have greater spiritual discernment, but we remain somewhat connected. However, through satanic rituals there is a seemingly sudden and complete separation of soul and spirit that then enables a person to see and hear demons.

In 1 Cor. 15:44 we read, *It is sown a natural body; it is raised a spiritual body. There is a natural body, and there is a spiritual body.* We know from this that we have a natural body and a spiritual body. It is through the natural body that we contact the physical world around us. We are not aware of having a spiritual body until we die and discard the natural body. This is as God intended. Somehow through rituals the Satanists use demons to separate the spiritual body from the natural body. When the soul and spirit have been separated and the natural body is separated from the spiritual body, then a person is fully aware of and enters into an entirely different dimension. This is the dimension I am calling the inner world. This world is vast and just as real to the individual as the physical world is to us. We think of spirits as being wispy, vapor-like beings, but those who are in this dimension tell me the demons have weight and substance.

The inner world is a world of demon spirits and alters and is accessed through the mind...more specifically through the imagination. Persons who get involved in Transcendental Meditation or seek spirit guides, for example, are using their imagination to contact the realm of evil spirits. God gave us an imagination. An imagination in itself is not an evil thing. We can use our imagination to envision a fabulous new invention that will be of great benefit to mankind. We can use our imagination to picture Jesus as he teaches his disciples and tells them to cast their nets down on the right side of the boat. An imagination can be used for good or it can be used for evil.

When ministering to the highly complex multiple there should come a time early in the sequence of memories where the person will become greatly distressed saying her right side seems to be separated from her left side. At this point a demon needs to be cast out. This will be helpful to the individual but will not deliver her from the spiritual dimension she experiences. This divided feeling may occur with a memory about the ceremony where the dividing was done. One woman described this ritual where the Satanists used the Hebrews 4:12 scripture in some twisted way while holding an actual sword over her and calling up demons to divide her.

Magic Surgery

Through magic surgery this spiritual world is furnished with various structures and objects. During magic surgery a child is hypnotized and/or drugged and told she is going to be operated on and a certain object is to be placed within her. The child knows what the object is and its purpose. The cultists cause the child to feel extreme pain in the area of the surgery, plenty of blood is spread around, the "incision" is made, the object "inserted", the incision "sewed up" and a bandage applied. For the rest of this person's life she believes this object is within her.

Because of the spiritual dimension she is in, she is able to see and experience this object as though it were a real thing in our three dimensional world. The Satanists use it for purposes of control.

For example, a child may be taken to Germany and shown a castle. She not only sees the outside of the castle but she is taken on a tour of the inside. She spends several days in the castle going through painful, terrifying rituals in many of the rooms. She is forced to memorize the castle's entire layout. There will be a small replica of the castle much like an architectural model or a small dollhouse... something three-dimensional that the child thoroughly learns. Once this has been memorized, she is subjected to magic surgery. A tiny replica of the castle is shown to the child and she is told that it is being placed inside. The castle is now "within" and has become a structure in the spiritual inner world. In this person's inner world she can now walk through the rooms and this castle has become as real to her in the spiritual dimension as it had been in the physical world.

In subsequent rituals, this person will dissociate many times and the alters formed will be assigned to live in various rooms. These rooms are guarded by demons, and booby traps are placed in strategic places so there is no escape for the alters locked in the rooms. These castles have cold, dark dungeons filled with rats and snakes along with torture rooms complete with all the medieval torture devices seen in our Hollywood movies.

This becomes an enormous scheme for control. If alters don't do exactly as told, they will be taken by demons to a torture chamber and tortured. This is extremely painful for the individual because the spiritual senses of her spiritual body are heightened. Spiritual senses are stronger than physical senses, I have been told. The pain even spreads to the physical body. When a spiritual helper has been willing to exchange his/her life for Christ's, there is tremendous authority given by the Lord over this whole scheme. Jesus knows how to protect the alters when they begin talking. He gives us power to lock up all the demons and He hides the alters where they cannot be found.

Through magic surgery the cultists have placed booby traps throughout the person's inner world. Of course, these things are not actually inside, but because the person believes they are there, demons can use them for control. Satanists anticipate the possibility that alters may begin talking to a counselor. To keep them silent in their rooms or to punish them for talking, the booby traps are in place to be triggered whenever any of the scheme is threatened. These booby traps can be anything a perverted, demon-filled mind can imagine. Think of any of the movies featuring Harrison Ford in the Indiana Jones series...these are the kinds of booby traps that can be in this inner world.

A very common booby trap device is a bomb. One particular afternoon I discovered that a woman who had just started having abuse memories had not had anything to drink that entire day. Upon inquiry the Lord revealed there was a bomb inside set to explode should she drink anything. She was absolutely terrified. I asked Him to remove it, which He did, and then she was able to drink two large glasses of water. In this inner world "what you *believe* is what you get." Demons can simulate the detonation of a bomb complete with sound effects and pain. Many of these devices are planned to destroy the life or sanity of the individual who begins talking. This is just one example of why this kind of spiritual help can only be successfully done by a Christian who lets Jesus Christ do the work. If a secular counselor tried to remove this bomb, it would have "exploded" and the woman would have needed medication and possibly hospitalization.

One lady described to me what happened inside when well meaning church people tried to cast demons out of her. A bomb exploded and she felt as though shrapnel had been propelled into every part of her body. The shrapnel was actually powerful demons catapulted into her arms, legs, head...every part of her body...with the message to kill those trying to help her and then run outside and jump in front of traffic. She was aware of what was happening but was totally out of control. Two men had been working with her, but at that point two more people were required to hold her down.

Anything in the physical world can be placed into a person's inner world through magic surgery. The following are some of the things commonly found in the inner world for purposes of control. These can only be removed as the Lord leads. Most of them are connected in some way to painful abuse memories and will be removed at the time of the memory; however, this is not always the case. It is important to let the Lord lead. It would not be good for a spiritual helper to randomly try to look for these devices.

1. Computers - The computer will be used by demons and/or cult alters to control anything or anybody in the system.
2. Receivers, walkie-talkies, etc. - The person may actually hear a perpetrator's voice giving her instructions. This is, of course, done by demons. If the perpetrator wants the person to come to a specific place at a certain time, he calls a demon to go activate the walkie-talkie and give the instructions to the individual. A demon has the ability to sound like and look like any human being.
3. Tape recorders - These may play demeaning, hurtful remarks said by other persons or they may play repeated instructions for certain behaviors, etc. These may be programmed to activate in any given circumstance. For example, if the person receives a compliment, a tape-recorded voice says demeaning things to negate anything kind that was said. Again, this is demonic trickery.
4. Video tapes - Horrific scenes of human torture, etc. can be repeatedly projected into the person's mind.
5. Alarm clocks - These can be set to sound off at different times during the night and also during the day to make sure the person never has restful sleep.
6. A furnace - This may be used to suck all the energy out of a person or suck alters into it for destruction. It may keep the person overheated. All of these are to keep the individual traumatized.
7. Mazes - Alters are often trapped behind mazes. Jesus is able to bring them out and destroy the maze.

These are only a few of the things that are commonly found in the inner world of the SRA. The possibilities are endless because anything in the physical world can be transferred into the inner world through trickery and magic surgery.

The Origin of Alters

For those persons born into families embroiled in generational Satanism, the abuse begins in their mother's womb. A fetus can be abused in many ways such as electric shock, needle jabs, bricks dropped on the mother's belly, raping the mother, etc. We assume a fetal monitor is used to measure the baby's heartbeat. When the heartbeat accelerates and then suddenly drops significantly, the baby has dissociated within the womb. The cultists try to get six, thirteen, or even eighteen splits in the womb since these are satanic numbers of power, but they are not always successful in getting these desired numbers. Each split in the womb then becomes a "seed" which will be further split to populate a layer of personalities within the inner structure of the person's psyche.

The Structure of the Inner World

The alters and furnishings of the inner world are not randomly placed. There is a basic structure into which each person or object is directed. This structure will have as many levels as there were splits in the womb. If a person split thirteen times in her mother's womb then her inner structure will have 13 levels. There are some instances where the number of splits *in utero* were not as many as desired, so immediately after birth the newborn baby was made to split once or twice adding to the number of levels.

These levels or layers should have a geometric shape that often is the same for each level. For example, if squares were used, each level may be a square. Others will have combinations of geometric figures such as squares combined with triangles or circles, for example. Each level is divided into sections or rooms where alters are assigned to live. Demon guards are stationed in strategic places on all the levels. Underneath all these layers will be a pit. Sometimes this pit will have as many levels as the basic structure itself.

The different levels are connected by staircases (often circular) that intersect the gates on each level. It is similar to a high-rise apartment building but the design may be more modernistic because the levels are not necessarily the same size and they may turn at different angles from one another. Often the levels are designed to rotate or spin.

This structure is "placed inside" the child at a very young age. A model of the structure is built and the child is required to thoroughly memorize it. She memorizes the structure including the location of demon guards on each level and the placement of the seed alter on each level. Then through magic surgery the structure is placed inside, and the child is told it will grow with her. During this "surgery" the child believes that she has been cut from her throat down to her lower abdomen and this structure then fills the entire trunk of her body.

Each alter formed through splits in the womb is assigned to a particular level. This alter on each level becomes the seed which populates through splitting that particular level of the structure. The top level of the structure is called the presenting level. This is where alters that perform the tasks of daily living are housed. They are the ones who clean the house, go to work, take care of the children, communicate with the outside world, etc. These alters are often unaware of each other until it is revealed to them through ministry. They know nothing about the alters on lower levels or that lower levels even exist. Upper level alters were formed by the victim for the purpose of coping with the challenges of everyday life and are sometimes called the "home system."

The presenting level will most likely have a small number of alters...perhaps as few as seven or eight. The area of this level will be the smallest of all levels. Progressing down through the structure we should expect to find increasingly larger and more densely populated levels. It is common for lower levels to have hundreds of alters. The lower the level the more committed to darkness the alters will probably be.

Cult alters living on the lower levels know all about the upper layers and are able to take control of the entire system. Those alters who are the most powerful and committed to darkness are on the lowest level. When lower level cult alters want to take over the body, they come up through the gates, give a password to each demon guarding the gates, and proceed to the top presenting level. The home system alters have no ability to resist the cult alters and are forced to do whatever they are told. Cult alters may take a home system alter down to a place of torture as punishment for talking or any other infringement. After a time of ministry it may be helpful to pray and ask the Lord to seal the gates so the lower level alters and demons cannot come up to the presenting level and cause trouble. This is not a formula...God has led me to do this with some persons but with others He has instructed me differently. We must be open to the Lord's guidance.

Kinds of Alters

Alters can be anyone or anything according to the desires of the programmers or according to the needs of the person. Someone who has been abused to this complexity knows only one coping mechanism...dissociation. By this means the cult purposely creates alters for their evil designs and the survivor on her own creates alters for coping with life. Therefore some alters will be cult alters with specific cult designated jobs and some alters will be helpers with jobs assigned by the abused person. There will also be alters who do not fall into either category which we will discuss later.

Cult alters were formed by the cult through rituals and torture to carry out the purposes of the cult. They have various duties such as teaching, storing information, performing rituals, taking her out to rituals, calling demons to her, storing satanic power, blocking ministry, managing programs, etc. In a highly complex multiple there will be numerous alters assigned to kill the survivor should she find effective Christian prayer ministry that begins setting her free.

Cult alters are given an identity by the cult complete with their own assigned physical characteristics. The survivor may be middle aged and overweight but an alter living within the same body may believe she is a teenager with a slim figure. Cult alters work against the well being of the individual even to the point of trying to kill her, so it is often necessary to tell them they inhabit the same body. This they often vehemently deny even saying demeaning things about the person's physical appearance and personality. At this point it is helpful to have them look into a mirror to prove to them they were deceived by the cult. It is common for them to proclaim that the mirror is a trick that they had been warned about. I tell them to stick out their tongue while looking in the mirror. This will often convince them they were deceived. Many of these will gladly relinquish their assignment of murder when they realize they would be committing suicide.

Satanists access the cult alters through the use of triggers such as code names, flashing lights, beeps, numbers, etc. Through abuse and programming the survivor actually becomes much like a human computer accessible to anyone who knows the program and the access codes. These alters can also be activated by other means. Some alters are activated by demons which the cult sends forth from their rituals. Other alters were formed and programmed years ago to become active on a certain date. For example, if the cult decided the person was to die at age 50, alters with the assignment to kill her would become active when she turned 50. Cult astrologers have known for eons when certain heavenly phenomena would occur. For example a full moon on the same day as a lunar eclipse occurring on Friday the 13th (which happened in March of 1998) was anticipated by the cults for many years. Certain alters may have been assigned to come forth on that day and take the person out to a ritual where these alters were to perform certain functions.

Each cult alter must be delivered of demons and converted to Jesus Christ. This is usually accomplished within fifteen to thirty minutes, more or less. Jesus gives them a new job and they become helpers working for the well being of the individual. Many of these cult alters have information which will be beneficial for reaching other alters. For example, a cult alter named Bobby attempted in my presence to kill the host person, but after conversion was assigned by Jesus the job of telling me whenever booby traps were nearby. Bobby had been forced by the cult to memorize the location of every booby trap on the first seven levels of the person's thirteen-tiered inner structure. Now that he was on our side he became a valuable asset to the ministry.

Other cult alters know they live in the host's body but still work against her. Some of these alters, which I call kamikaze alters, are so committed to darkness they will gladly sacrifice their own life to kill the survivor. Some of these will be won to Jesus Christ, but others comprised of pure sin nature will not, even though they see and hear Him. These Jesus removes.

A woman with highly complex DID/MPD will have many male alters. They may appear early in the ministry or they may not manifest until several months of ministry have been completed, but they will definitely be there.

It is common to meet an alter who believes she is a dog. She may not be able to speak but can only bark. Asking another alter who may be watching to speak for her is helpful. How, one may ask, does someone come to believe she is dog? Satanists like to make their victims feel inhuman. The less human they feel the more willing they will be to welcome the demons and adopt their behavior (demons can be very animalistic). This kind of programming is very brutal. They make a child or teenager strip naked and put her in a pen with dogs for perhaps as long as a week. She is not allowed to display any human behavior during that entire week. She is forbidden to stand up on two feet, speak, sleep on a bed, drink or eat with her hands. She must crawl on her hands and knees and lap water and food from a dish as the dogs do. Male dogs repeatedly rape her.

Some alters may be kittens. I have found these alters to have been formed by the survivor in her attempts to cope with her abuse. One little girl alter told me she noticed that the kittens on her family's farm were left alone. She reasoned that perhaps if she could become a kitten her abusers would leave her alone. Some of these alters will speak as well as meow, but others will require someone else to speak for them. Once I was ministering to a kitten alter who would gently meow and rub her head against my shoulder. Then she would suddenly act like an angry cat hissing and clawing at her face. It took a minute before I realized she had demons that were also acting like a cat.

Some alters, due to abusive programming, may believe they are space aliens or robots. One woman remembered being subjected to a week of dog programming, followed by a week of alien programming, followed by another week of robot programming. By the end of those three weeks she had no idea what she was, but she was sure she was not human.

One of the most memorable alters I've met was Rubber Man. He, as part of the home system, was created by the survivor to fulfill the incredible work demands forced on her by her wicked stepmother. Being made of rubber, he could stretch his arms and legs to reach into unreachable places and accomplish seemingly impossible tasks. As he was sharing about himself he kept stretching out his arms and legs to show how he could reach things. He was particularly good at washing windows and cleaning out gutters. Rubber Man never talked...he only sang in a loud voice making everything rhyme. He liked to cheer her when she felt sad.

Many alters, especially baby and child alters, will have no particular job. They may be locked away in dark dungeons, pits, prisons, nurseries, etc. where they are frightened and miserable. These alters are often the "cast offs" formed as the person was subjected to increasing degrees of pain and terror during programming or rituals. In order to produce the desired cult alter, the Satanists will subject a person to excruciating horror and pain necessitating several dissociations, each subsequent alter being stronger and more committed to darkness than the previous one. For example, if the person switches five times before the desired alter is formed, the first four alters are not wanted by the cult. These are then assigned a living death in some type of prison.

Sometimes an alter who is perceptively very little will manifest but won't answer any questions. Chances are this is a preverbal alter. Ask if someone else can speak for her. Yesterday I met a preverbal alter in a 53-year-old woman. With her hair pulled down over her face, she peeked out at me while sucking her thumb and rubbing the top of her nose with her forefinger. She was obviously frightened but curious. When she wouldn't answer any questions, I asked if someone could speak for her. At that point I met 11-year-old Lisa who told me all about "Rini's" abuse. Rini then returned and I asked Jesus to minister to her. As I had anticipated she was afraid of Jesus, but as He often does, He sent a little lamb to her. I watched as she petted the lamb and giggled when he nuzzled against her neck. After a short time with the lamb, she looked up into Jesus' face with total awe and then lifted her arms for Him to pick her up. She seemed to relax and rest her head upon His shoulder as He carried her away to a safe place.

CHAPTER TEN

MINISTERING TO ALTERS

Basically everyone is aware of the battle between good and evil, not only in the world, but also within. It is often depicted in cartoons by a person with a devil whispering into one ear and an angel whispering into the other. When one becomes a Christian he/she should experience an intensifying of that inward battle because the light of Christ has entered his/her being and that light begins exposing the darkness of the sin nature within. This battle is not a pleasant experience and we, as Christians, long for a time when the inward struggle will cease, and we will enter into a rest in Christ. This is not to say we long for death, but we do desire for Jesus Christ to reign in our hearts to such an extent that peace and rest dominate our souls.

For SRA persons who have made a commitment to Jesus Christ, this battle is intensified exceedingly to the extent they experience having a dark side and a light side. Their dark side has, through satanic rituals, made vows to serve Satan. Their light side is committed to Jesus Christ...and the battle rages.

During the course of ministry the alters on the light side need to be protected from demons and cult alters, and the alters on the dark side need to be brought to a commitment to Jesus Christ. There seems to be some confusion about this in the counseling community. I have heard counselors, for whom I have the utmost respect, say it is not necessary to bring alters to a commitment to Christ. However, if peace is ever to come within the SRA person in this life, the dark side must be brought to the light--one alter at a time or sometimes in groups.

Every Christian should be aware of the process in his own soul of Christ (light) increasing within as the individual (darkness of the sin nature) decreases (John 3:30). This is the process of sanctification. As we read in Phil. 2:12b,13: *work out your own salvation with fear and trembling. For it is God which worketh in you both to will and to do of his good pleasure.* When a person's soul is broken and divided as in SRA/DID, we need to help them through this process. It is God who does the work; we are there as co-laborers with Him.

The Satanists who terrorize their chosen child are aware of this light and darkness within and use it to their advantage. They are able, through the torture of the rituals, to cause a person to split several times until an alter is formed who consists of nothing but pure sin nature. This alter will be totally committed to Satan and the cult and will gladly carry out any orders she is given. She will have powerful demons attached to her to empower her in her task. She is then placed in her designated place within the structure (probably on a very low level) where she will wait until the time the cult signals her to come forth. Fulfilling her task is her sole purpose in life; she knows nothing else. Her entire identity lies in successfully completing her assignment. This kind of alter will never surrender to Christ.

In a ritual purposed for the creation of this kind of alter (these are seldom child alters but more often teens or young adults), a person is told she must do something unspeakably, nauseatingly grotesque. She refuses to do it. To obtain her compliance, the cult subjects her to merciless torture until she splits into someone who can endure the torment more effectively. When this alter can no longer endure it, another alter is formed to take more pain. Eventually, after several splits, an alter will be formed out of rage, hatred and pure sin nature who will gladly do whatever grotesque task is demanded of her. She vows total allegiance to Satan and is fully committed to the cult's objectives.

This kind of alter is the personification of the "old man" (Romans 6:1-6). We all have sin of this dimension within us, but because it is mixed with the good, we don't recognize it and we can subdue it. In SRA it is isolated, split off from the main stream of consciousness and given a name.

Not all SRA persons will manifest this kind of alter. It may be that Jesus just quietly deals with them rather than have the minister bother with them since they are not redeemable. These kinds of alters are sometimes assigned to kill the host person should she begin coming out of the cult's control through spiritual Christian ministry. However, there are alters with suicide assignments who are redeemable. The spiritual director, through the Holy Spirit's guidance, must discern carefully in these situations. If the alter consists of pure sin nature and is not redeemable, she will simply disappear after her demons have been cast out. Most alters will come to Jesus and repent of their sins.

We need to realize, as Christian spiritual directors, that this same sin nature resides in each of us. This means the potential for heinous acts of sin dwells in us too. Had we been subjected to different circumstances in life, parts of us could have been committed to darkness also if it were not for the love and protection of Jesus Christ. This understanding helps us approach SRA ministry with compassion and humility. It also helps us understand that the process of transformation we see graphically depicted in the SRA person is also occurring in us in less perceptible ways.

Jesus Christ allows each of us to spend time in the "furnace of affliction" (Isa. 48:10) that He may separate that which is redeemable in us (silver or gold) from the sin nature (dross) which He eventually destroys. The SRA person is taken through the "furnace of affliction" resulting in the separating of the sin nature which projects its own persona. This becomes the unredeemable alter who is totally subservient to the cult. When Jesus deals with this kind of alter, the alter just disappears even as the sin in us disappears when we die to self and repent of our sin. Other alters will be taken to a safe place or be integrated with the core personality.

The Safe Place

Each alter to whom we minister will need to know where she belongs. It would not be safe for her to return to her formerly assigned place in the inner structure where the cult had placed her. Jesus will integrate some alters immediately after their memories are processed. Other alters are not ready for integrating because they need more time for maturing and healing. These Jesus will take to a safe place prepared by Him where demons and cult alters cannot come. Still others will not be merged until a later time because they still have a job to do to help the host personality (the person who has come to you for help). These will remain within the inner structure but secretly hidden by Jesus until He calls them forth to help with the ministry.

An example of this latter type of alter would be Nancy, an alter who held the keys to all the programs on this person's 18 levels. Nancy's cult job was to unlock the rooms to destructive programs whenever the cult activated her. She had free access to all the levels in the structure and the demon guards would always let her pass. After she received ministry and accepted Jesus as her savior, He hid her in a maze within the structure so He could call her forth whenever He wanted any programming revealed for ministry. Of course, Jesus could unlock the programming rooms without her, but alters like to feel important and need a job to replace their old one, so that is how Jesus handled her. This also helps parts of this person's identity (alter) help other parts of her identity so she is learning to allow these parts to work together rather than work against each other.

All the alters have been brutally abused...one could rightly say they have lived through hell; therefore, the safe place where Jesus takes them is correspondingly like heaven. (Remember this all takes place in a dimension unknown to the rest of us who have not experienced the occult practices which remove the veil as explained in the previous chapter.) Usually the babies and young children are taken to one place and the older children and teens to another.

The safe place for young children might be a lovely cottage near a babbling brook with big trees to climb and little animals such as puppies, kittens and lambs with which to play. The young children may get to help with the babies in the cottage nursery or perhaps tend the lambs. Adult alters who love children may be there to supervise. Angels stand guard so the children have nothing to fear, and Jesus comes from time to time to play with them and give them lots of hugs and affirmation. The children need to play. Many SRA children were never allowed to play. Play is a very vital part of childhood--without it we cannot develop normally. This is a place of healing. At some point when enough healing has transpired, all the children will be integrated with the original person (the person created by God before abuse began). Only Jesus knows when this time will be. He initiates it and we stand back in awe and amazement at the wonderful healing only He can do.

The teens will usually be in a different place that corresponds to their needs and desires. I remember one woman's safe place for the teens was a log cabin in the mountains near a lake. Jesus also comes here and ministers to them and the angels are watching over them. When they are ready, they too will be integrated. This may be done as a group. For example, Jesus may have them line up and have the last person in line step into the one ahead of her, and that one step into the next one, etc. and then the last person steps into the original person and the integrating of that group is completed. Jesus has many different ways of doing things and we must always leave this to Him. We are not to decide when they are to be merged or how it is done.

Encouraging the Alters to Manifest

Secular counselors may use hypnosis to reach a person's alters but as Christian ministers we don't want to use this technique. To do so would be to take control of the ministry process, and we want Jesus to be in control. The alters should be reached through prayer. Only Jesus knows when they are ready to talk, and He alone knows who needs to speak first.

The alters are more likely to speak once a relationship of trust and love has developed with the spiritual friend. This is one reason SRA/DID is more difficult to heal in a professional counseling environment where the delimitation of time is a major factor. Some persons' alters will respond in that setting but others will not. People do need appointments to meet with me, but my office is presently in my home, and I allow plenty of time for developing relationship. We may walk around the yard and look at the flowers after a time of ministry, or I will sometimes take someone to lunch. I offer them a cup of tea and chat in the kitchen for a while. I call them at home to see how they are. Many of the women I minister to attend our church, so I see them at church and also in our home groups. When trust and love are established, the alters are often standing in line waiting their chance to talk (figuratively speaking).

Usually the more desirous of healing the survivor is, the more easily the alters will be reached. First we pray together inviting the presence of the Lord to be with us, guiding us in all we do. (It is important for the spiritual director to keep his/her eyes open during prayer because the survivor could be doing any number of strange things, if demons or alters manifest, and needs our constant awareness.) We confess that we can do nothing ourselves but Christ can do all things. We pray for a while about how loving and kind Jesus is and thanking Him that He is with us. We ask Him to reveal anything the person needs to know in order to get better. At this point some persons will begin having a memory. The memory may be told by the host personality as the alters speak to her, or the individual alters may speak directly to the spiritual director. Some persons will have an entire memory with crying and releasing of emotions but will be unable to speak. In such situations the spiritual director must pray silently and wait until it is over and the person can relate what was happening.

Other persons won't have a memory with this approach. I had one woman who only had a memory when I prayed over her in tongues. The Baptism of the Holy Spirit (Acts 2; 10:44-48; 19:1-7; 1 Cor. 12; 14) is invaluable in SRA/DID ministry. There have been many times when I didn't know what to do so I just prayed in the Spirit. (There are many times in this ministry when the spiritual helper will be totally baffled about what is happening and won't know what to do. For example, what do you do when a person suddenly passes out in front of you?) This releases the Holy Spirit to do whatever needs to be done. Speaking in tongues is also a powerful weapon against the demons.

One woman only had memories when I read the Bible to her. We would turn to the Psalms or some other passage she had in mind and as I read, the memories would begin.

It is quite common for memories to begin surfacing just prior to the ministry time. It could be in a dream the night before or in a sudden flash of memory while driving to the meeting for ministry, etc. Sometimes bits and pieces of memory will show up in the person's journal a day or two prior to our meeting.

I encourage my SRA friends to keep a journal and record in it each day's significant events, emotions, dreams, scriptural insights, etc. Sometimes as they write, alters begin communicating with one another and even demons may write messages. Pieces of memory may come out in this process and it also provides a good release for emotions. Many abused persons express themselves beautifully in poetry. Some who have never written poetry may find they are gifted in this area as they keep their daily journal. I make sure they understand that I may want to see the journal from time to time. Sometimes distinct changes in handwriting are evident which may be an aid in determining whether or not a person has dissociated.

Once persons begin having memories, they may find there are certain "triggers" that cause parts of memory to surface. For example, they may have difficulty attending church because the minister's robe, the candlesticks, or other religious articles may remind them of rituals. Many SRA persons were subjected to rituals in churches.

It is not unusual for women I help to have a memory surface in our church on Sunday morning even though my husband doesn't wear a robe and we have no candlesticks. (We have tried to remove some of the religious items that could make SRA persons uncomfortable in our church.) It may be that the atmosphere of love and the Lord's presence in church causes a person's defensive walls to weaken, and the Holy Spirit is then able to push up a memory. He knows I can take her into the office and minister to her during the sermon.

I like to think of memory as occurring on three levels: the emotional level, the cognitive level and in the physical body (body memory). Body memory is a strange phenomenon for which I have no explanation except to say marks (e.g. red marks or bruises) will sometimes appear on a person's body that correspond exactly to the memory. Sometimes there are no marks or bruises, but the person feels physical pain corresponding to the memory. It is most beneficial when a memory transpires on all three levels at the same time. Sometimes a memory will start on only one level. For example, someone may arrive at your office with bruises on her legs for which she has no explanation, but when she has her memory (cognitively and emotionally) the bruises will correspond exactly to the memory. At other times a person will feel an emotion, panic for example, and have no explanation as to why she feels this way. When the cognitive memory comes it will correspond to the panic, and after the memory the panic will be gone. Sometimes there is cognitive memory with no emotions. The emotions will be released at a later time. In these cases it is important to pray for Jesus to push up the buried emotions.

Ministry for a Ritual Memory

When assisting someone through a ritual memory, it is helpful to remember that it may have taken several alters to get through one ritual. The memory may progress rapidly with the person obviously switching from alter to alter as it proceeds with each successive alter being progressively stronger in her ability to fulfill the cult's demands. If this is the case, Jesus will minister to all the alters after the entire memory is completed. At that time He may minister to each one individually or He may minister to them as a group.

Some memories will progress more slowly and stop after each alter tells her part. Jesus may minister to each alter and take her to the safe place before the next alter surfaces to give her account. The spiritual director needs discernment to know when the entire memory is over. It might be harmful for a person to leave with the memory only partially completed because she would not have peace, and the rest of it might surface with no one present to help. The majority of ritual memories culminate in the rape of the SRA person which helps us know when we've reached the end of the memory. Sometimes there is more after the rape, so we need to enquire of the Lord before assuming the memory is over.

All alters need to know who Jesus is and make a decision for Him or against Him. If the survivor has been a Christian for several years, many of her alters will know who Jesus is and some will have accepted Him as Savior. Others will have rejected Him. Many unmet alters will have been observing the spiritual helper's ministry to the others and some of these, on their own, may have come to believe in Jesus. I've seen these alters surface with something important to say but ask to pray for salvation before telling me their information. In certain persons the alters who have come to know Jesus are so excited they evangelize some of the others.

The cult often does extensive programming to keep their victim separated from God. She may have been severely punished for praying or reading a Bible. Someone dressed up like Jesus may have beaten or raped her. Because of this she will have alters who make it difficult for her to pursue a relationship with God. These alters are usually easily brought to Jesus when they see Him. He will do something for them that wipes away their misconceptions. This kind of programming is usually extensive. Dealing with one or two alters with this kind of programming will not release the survivor to freely pursue God. She may have many alters who are working against her in this area. As the ministry progresses, all of these will eventually be released from their programming.

Some alters, particularly the youngest ones, may be afraid of Jesus because they have been so abused by men, and Jesus, of course, is a man. With these Jesus will do something to alleviate their fears. He may send a gentle little lamb to nuzzle them as He stands in the distance as the good shepherd. This calms their fears, and they are then willing to go with Him. Sometimes they'll ask me first if it is all right to go with Him. Of course, babies and children too young to understand the Gospel don't need to have it all explained to them; they just go with Jesus.

The most difficult alters to deal with are the cult alters who have found their identity and purpose in serving the Devil. These will want nothing to do with Jesus. They, of course, are totally deceived and we need to set them free from their deception. We can never argue them out of their stance because human reasoning will have no effect on them. There must be an intervention by the Holy Spirit that we can help to arrange.

First we ascertain what this alter's basic issue is. It could be fear, guilt, power, etc. and then we ask Jesus to demonstrate how He is the answer to that issue. For example, many alters don't want to come to Jesus because they believe all the power is in their master, Satan. They believe they have great satanic powers that they don't want to forfeit. They may have been told Jesus is weak or dead. It is necessary to create some kind of showdown where the supremacy of Jesus over Satan is proven.

The Holy Spirit will guide the spiritual helper in these interventions but here are a few I've found to be successful:

Intervention: An alter manifests in the survivor and says she doesn't like the way I'm interfering in the cult's plans. She says she is taking the person out now and starts to get out of her chair to leave. I reach over and hold her down. She tells me to get my hands off so I say, "Okay, if you don't want me to touch you, I'll ask Jesus to hold you there." She will struggle and strain trying to get out of the chair but won't be able to. I'm not touching her...the Lord is holding her in the chair. This usually makes her very angry, but at this point we can talk about power. I may say something like, "If Satan is so powerful, and he is your master, why don't you ask him to help you?" She will call on Satan, and, of course, he doesn't come, so she calls on her demon "friends" to assist her. (These are the demons assigned to this alter during the rituals...there may be two, six, or even more of these demons which surface at various times during ministry to this alter.) One of her demons will surface sounding very threatening and warning me to stay out of their business. I cast him out and another one manifests trying to sound more powerful than the first. After these are dealt with, the alter will really be fuming. At this point I tell her she has been deceived and tell her about Jesus. She will often reject the Gospel and claim she will be loyal to Satan forever. I keep talking about Jesus and then say something like, "They hurt you, didn't they. You took the pain and did what they told you because the others were too weak. You did a good job, but Jesus has something better for you. Jesus, would you please let her feel your love and peace for 15 seconds?" She obviously feels this as evidenced by the look on her face. I tell her she can feel this way any time she wants if she'll renounce darkness and ask Jesus into her heart. She may protest that she has made vows to serve Satan. I tell her she can renounce them. As she starts to renounce darkness more demons manifest and all remaining demons are removed. Then she breaks her vows, renounces darkness and prays the sinner's prayer. At this point the Lord may talk to her for a while, and she'll confess her sins and ask His forgiveness. Then she leaves with Jesus and the host person returns.

Intervention: A cult alter vows to be loyal to Satan forever. I tell her she is deceived and relate to her the truth of the

Gospel. She rejects it. I ask Jesus to show her where she will go if she continues to follow Satan. Jesus shows her hell. She still insists on her loyalty to darkness. I ask Jesus to show her where she will go if she should choose to renounce darkness and believe in Him. She sees heaven. She still vows her allegiance to Satan. Then I ask the Lord to let her experience hell. She then feels the pain of the fires of hell and cries out while beating herself as though trying to extinguish the flames. I say, "If Satan is such a good master, ask him to save you." She calls on Satan, and he does nothing. I tell her there is only one who can save her and His name is Jesus. As soon as she says "Jesus," He releases her from the pain of hell. Usually this alter is ready to accept the fact that she has been deceived and will ask Jesus into her heart. Of course, demons manifest from time to time until they are all removed from this alter. Jesus will minister to her for a while, and then take her with Him.

Intervention: Some cult alters have experienced so much hell in this life they are not impressed with the fires of hell; therefore, the above intervention will have no effect on them. These alters may be won through love. At this point I have asked Jesus to let them experience hell, but they have chosen to remain in it rather than call upon His name. Jesus only leaves them there a short time because they obviously aren't going to respond. When this happens, I may ask Jesus to let them feel his love and peace for a few seconds. Sometimes the Lord leads me to talk gently to them about Jesus and His love, telling them I love them too as I softly caress their face. This is frightening to them as they have never been treated kindly by anyone. The only touch they've ever known has been abusive. They may protest saying it is frightening and different, but I continue stroking their face and talking about love and then watch them melt. (This is the love of Christ... not our human love... coming through the spiritual helper, and love truly is the most powerful force in the universe!) They are ready then to meet the Lord, and He will talk with them and bring them to repentance and salvation.

Intervention: I ask a cult alter if she continually hears voices degrading her or telling her what to do. She'll answer in the affirmative. I ask her if she ever tires of the voices, and she'll say yes. I then ask if she has ever been able to make the voices stop, and she'll say no. I then ask Jesus to make the voices cease for 10 or 15 seconds, which He does. She is surprised and impressed. I tell her that Jesus loves her and has the power to set her free. She gives her heart to the Lord.

It is often helpful to ask a cult alter if there is anything that bothers her. If there is, you can ask the Lord to demonstrate that He is able to meet her need whatever it may be. This will often win her to the Lord. Of course, she must always repent of her sin, renounce her vows, renounce darkness and ask Jesus into her heart.

Interaction of Alters

Some alters will be locked away somewhere all alone. Other alters will interact with each other. The cult alters terrorize the children and do many destructive things to the friendly alters and the host person. Many alters have programming jobs assigned by the cult that involve doing things to other alters. This will be explained more thoroughly in the chapter on programming.

When a child's basic needs are not met in childhood, she will often create alters to meet those needs. For example, a child who needs a mother's love but receives none may create an alter who is a mother figure. This alter will love the other alters and do all the things the child desires from her mother but never receives. I remember one such alter named "Mammy." She was described as looking like "Aunt Jemima" on the syrup bottle. She loved and cared for many of the child alters.

There may be alters who are caretakers and help the younger, more frightened child alters. I remember Jimmy. He was a big brother who protected the children and did things to hide them when they were threatened by demons or cult alters.

Internal Self-Helpers

During ministry an alter may manifest who knows many helpful things about the needs of the other alters and who gives helpful insights from time to time. These alters are called "internal self-helpers." I remember one named "Ancient One" and another named "Mentor." They seemed to possess many basic understandings about the person's life that were essentially important for the person's healing. They were never taken to a safe place or given an assignment by Jesus...they were just always there helping in any way they could. Sometimes the information they offered contained such wisdom and insight I wondered if they might have been angels manifesting in the person. Who knows? One sees many strange things in this ministry for which there seems to be no explanation.

The Original Person

At some point the spiritual helper will meet someone who is the original person...the one who existed before the abuse began. This person is often pre-verbal and may even be found floating in the amniotic fluid of her mother's womb since SRA commonly begins in the mother's womb. Even persons not ritually abused may have dissociated in the womb. For example, a drunken father could have beaten the pregnant mother causing her to fall down a flight of stairs. The traumatized baby could have dissociated in the womb at that time.

One of the alters may speak for her or the host person will relate to the spiritual helper what she is seeing. All of this would be impossible without the supernatural working of the Holy Spirit. The Lord will minister sovereignly to the original person and take her to a unique safe place apart from the alters where she will receive special ministry from the Lord. She may manifest and talk to the spiritual helper from time to time.

In most cases after the original person has been found, the host person will be cognizant of her and her progress as she ages and matures over the duration of the ministry. When the original person has reached the level of growth, maturity and healing determined by the Lord, all other parts will be integrated into her. All of this is determined by the Lord not the spiritual helper.

In SRA the original person is often found between level one and level two on the underneath side of the first level of the inner structure. When this is the case, she will be found early in the ministry and can be observed by the host person as she grows. However, this is not always the case. One woman I ministered to had 18 levels in her upper structure and 18 levels in the pit. The Lord led us in ministry over the course of about three years down through the upper 18 levels but when we reached the pit, He took us to the lowest level, level 36, and we ministered from the bottom of the pit upwards. As we reached the first level in the pit (level 19 actually) we found the original person just underneath it between the first and second levels of the pit.

Although it took three years for the original person to be found, the Lord had kept her concealed and protected. When we found her, I witnessed one of the most astonishing things I have ever seen in this ministry. This woman, the host person, got out of her chair and laid on her back on the floor in front of me with her legs in the birthing position. She began to pant and grunt as she went through the labor of giving birth. Suddenly she changed and began to cry like a newborn infant.

After a few seconds of this she was a one-year-old looking around and saying "Dada, Mama." I watched with my mouth wide open in amazement as she went through all the different stages of growth before my eyes. At the end of it she was walking around the room as an adult making plans for her future. Even though I had not found the original person until quite late in the ministry, God had been sovereignly ministering to her, and she had been growing and maturing all along. She had started as a fetus in the womb and grown to adulthood without my survivor friend or me knowing about it. God was working mightily. He allowed this manifestation of growth so we could see what had taken place. Not long after this, the woman's many alters began integrating into the original person who was now mature enough for integration to commence.

In ministry the Lord does not necessarily take us down through the levels consecutively. There is, however, a general direction of starting from the top and working down to the pit. When the pit is reached, He may start from the top of the pit and work downward or He may start at the bottom and work upward. When dealing with programming, it is not uncommon to meet one alter on each level during one ministry session. This will be described more fully in the chapter on programming.

Core Personalities

Some alters are mere fragments or pieces of personality. However, other personalities, the core personalities, contain the very essence or center of being of the person. These personalities contain the person's true self in divided form. The alters that are personality fragments will never be seen again once they have received ministry and been taken by Jesus to a safe place. The core personalities, however, will remain and present to the spiritual director from time to time. They continue to grow and mature until such a time, determined by Jesus, when they integrate into the original person. The personality fragments are first integrated into the core personalities, and then the core personalities in turn integrate into the original person.

Cutting

Sometimes abused persons will purposely cut themselves. They may use a knife, scissors, jagged glass or any other sharp instrument. The cuts may be in visible places such as arms or legs, or they may be on parts of the body covered with clothing. Sometimes these cuts are in the shape of an upside down cross or some other satanic symbol. Many times there is no particular shape to the cuts.

There are several reasons for cutting in the SRA person. Sometimes the demon of mutilation is manifesting and driving the person to cut. There are also alters who have the job of cutting. The cult may have programmed her for cutting so that in the event she started talking, someone would see her cuts and insist she be hospitalized. Once she was in a hospital they could access her to punish her or reprogram her. I've seen demons manifesting and digging into the cuts with her fingernails trying to embed germs leading to an infection that would require hospitalization.

For some people, cutting becomes a coping mechanism. When the emotional pain is unbearable, the physical pain, which seems less painful, will distract from the intolerable inner agony.

When life seems totally out of control, cutting makes them feel in control. The thinking goes something like this: "I can do anything to my body I want to and no one can stop me. I have authority over my own body." This is comforting to someone who has been totally controlled by her family and the cult.

There are times when their confusion is so great, they're not sure if they are dead or alive. If they cut and see blood flowing, they know they are alive. This seems comforting.

Maps

In some persons there will be alters who have memorized maps indicating the location of some of the alters or the structure of the inner world. Should you meet one of these alters, she would be able to draw a map for you which would reveal interesting and helpful things about the system.

I caution spiritual directors not to go seeking the maps. If they are needed, Jesus will have them presented to you. If not, you will be taking the ministry process into your own hands by seeking them. Maps are fascinating. It is exciting to see someone draw one of these maps, but we must leave this in the hands of the Holy Spirit.

Maps are not always necessary for successful ministry to even the most highly complex and highly programmed SRA person. Maps can actually slow the ministry process. Jesus can have them show you a map and you can call each alter out by name, or Jesus may not show you the map and He may bring them all out in a group without your ever seeing the map. The second way is faster.

Maps should be in neat, geometrical shapes. Any map that looks like a diagram for a buried treasure hunt may be a fake map designed to lead the spiritual helper to a booby trap that could injure the person.

A Word About Guidance

I approach every prayer-ministry time by faith with no preconceived plan of action. I usually feel inadequate knowing I can do nothing but believing "I can do all things through Christ who strengthens me." I am the human agent in authority over the ministry process, but I am totally dependent on the Holy Spirit. I seldom have visions. I have never seen an angel or Jesus. I don't hear voices. I FEEL common and ungifted because I do only those things that come into my mind which seem like my own thoughts. Over the years I've come to know this is the way God leads me. I used to find this frustrating because my SRA friend was seeing and hearing in a dimension that is closed to me. I wanted God to bring me into that dimension too, but so far, He hasn't. I can see by the results of the ministry that He doesn't need to bring me into that realm. My inability to see and hear these things keeps me totally dependent on the Holy Spirit. The closer our walk with Jesus the more our thoughts are aligned with His and the stronger His guidance will be.

I say this to encourage the reader that I am not walking in some realm or dimension of supernatural manifestations. I walk by faith. God doesn't say to me, "Today I'm going to have you dealing with alters on level six." What happens is I pray and ask God what He wants to do for the survivor that day. When an alter manifests in the person and begins talking, I find out where she is and what her problems are. God brings the alter to me and then I use my understanding of Scripture and basic ministry goals to help her.

It is important to ask the Lord questions as you minister in SRA. I am constantly confronted with situations I don't understand and often talk to the Lord out loud as I minister.

CHAPTER ELEVEN

DEALING WITH DEMONS

People who have been satanically ritually abused will have demons in them because the central purpose of the rituals is to fill them with demons (powers); therefore, it is impossible to successfully minister in this area without dealing with demons.

Some Christians believe a Christian cannot have a demon; however, I do not see this in the Scriptures. If we think about it, it would not be fair to many abused people if this were the case. If a newborn baby is dedicated to Satan and subjected to painful rituals over which it has no control for the purpose of demon possession, are we to say that person can never become a Christian until all the demons are cast out? All the women to whom I have ministered for SRA have been Christians. They love Jesus and are as committed to Him as they are able to be apart from the alters whom we may not have met yet...ones who may have made a commitment to darkness during extreme duress. As little children, isolated and abused, they cried out for Jesus many times, and He was with them helping them bear the emotional and physical pain of SRA. If the demon possessed man of Gadara in Mark 5 was able to worship Jesus while the Legion was still in him, certainly SRA people can worship Him too.

According to the Bible, God has given Christians authority and power over demons. The Greek word for authority, *exou-*

sia, is also translated power, so we may use these words inter-changeably. All Christians have this authority to some extent but our power over the demons is directly commensurate to our walk with Jesus. This power increases as Jesus increases in us. The more authority Jesus has over our heart the more authority we will have over the demons and over the alters too. It is like the centurion in Matthew 8:9 who said, ... *I am a man under authority, having soldiers under me: and I say to this man, Go, and he goeth; and to another, Come, and he co-meth; and to my servant, Do this, and he doeth it.* The more we grow in faith, die to self, and pour ourselves out for others the more authority we will have. Power is not something we pos-sess; it comes from the very life of Christ within us; however, for our purposes here we may refer to having power or being given power.

In Matthew 10:1 we read, *And when he had called unto him his twelve disciples, he gave them power against unclean spirits, to cast them out...* It is important we notice he gave this power to his *disciples* but not to the multitudes. There are multitudes who profess to believe in Jesus today, but not all of them are disciples. To be a disciple of Jesus we must be willing to make sacrifices to follow Him as did His disciples of old. As we grow in our faith and commitment to the Lord, we become His disciples, and He imparts to us the authority we need to cast out demons.

Committing to ministry in the area of SRA entails sacrifice because it requires much time and patience. I am convinced these are the most wounded people on earth and they deserve our sacrifice. The Bible tells us in Matt. 25:31-46 that when we minister to the least of our brethren we have done so to Jesus. To commit to the SRA prayer ministry but be unwilling to sacrifice the necessary time could result in partially healed persons who could subsequently suffer more severe problems. To believe one is healed of SRA only to have it crop up again a year or two after termination of ministry could cause deep despair in an individual. If one is called to SRA ministry, then one should be committed to give all the time necessary to ensure a person is totally healed. This will require forsaking some of our own pursuits, but the rewards are immense. Not only do we have the reward of seeing a desperate person totally transformed into a new life of victory, but we, ourselves, are transformed into a new dimension in Jesus Christ. There are no words to express my gratitude to God for calling me into this ministry. The rewards have far exceeded any sacrifices I have made.

Only when we are willing to make the sacrifices necessary to be a disciple will we have the power to deal with the demons encountered in SRA. These demons are not the "personal" demons that come on people because they enter into sin. These demons are deliberately called into people for the purpose of power. These are the demons listed in Eph. 6:12: *For we wrestle not against flesh and blood, but against principalities, against powers, against the rulers of the darkness of this world, against spiritual wickedness in high places.* When we enter into ministry with prayer, the Lord determines which demons we are able to handle and allows them to manifest. If we are not spiritually strong enough to handle one, the Lord will keep him locked up. As we continue in deliverance ministry, the Lord will give us increasing amounts of power over the demons.

I remember one particular Halloween when the Lord said I would be up all night ministering to a certain lady and that during the course of the night, He would give me two new levels of power. (Many SRA persons have alters and demons programmed to take them out to rituals on certain occasions-- Halloween being one of them.) That night I had a queen size mattress on the family room floor where we rested from time to time and battled demons. Her husband was on the couch beside the mattress. All night long cult alters and powerful demons manifested. The first group of demons was so strong they were pulling her husband and me off the mattress onto the floor as we tried to hold her down while exorcizing them. There were two groups with this amount of power. The next group I was able to control myself with very little effort. I realized the demons were not less powerful but that I had received a new level of power. Then two or three more groups surfaced that were dragging us across the room. The next group I was able to handle easily alone. I had received another level of power. If I had not been willing to make the sacrifice of forfeiting a night's rest, I would not have received that power (the power being an increase of Christ in me) but beyond that I would have been unwilling to make the sacrifice requested by Jesus. It would have been my loss. That was fourteen years ago. The levels of power have been increasing steadily ever since.

Not long after that the Lord gave me a new power to deal with the demons in groups. Severely ritually abused people will have an enormous number of demons. Their bodies are weakened and sometimes diseased due to their abuse, and the manifesting in their bodies of the demons can be exhausting. The Lord said I could have the person visualize the demons as I ask Him to line them up, link them together, roll them into a ball, shrink it down tiny, and send it out. We usually bring out the strongman first and then his workers are brought out in a ball. This is not a technique--this is a power and can only be used when the Lord indicates the spiritual director has matured to this level. There are certain powerful demons that I have not been able to do this with. These must be brought out individually. The Lord will lead the spiritual director in all this and will only bring forth the demons He knows he/she is capable of handling...the rest He sovereignly handles.

The Gadarene Demoniac

A frequently asked question is, "Why don't you cast out all the demons at once like Jesus did with the Legion?" (Mark 5). This question reveals a certain naiveté amongst believers concerning the power of demonic beings. Until one starts doing deliverance, one doesn't understand the power of these things; they are immensely powerful. Yes, Jesus' power is far greater, but we only possess small amounts of that power. Jesus had the power to walk on water, change water into wine and raise the dead (amongst other things). Most of us aren't there yet. I believe we will be at some point because the Word tells us, "He that believeth on me, the works that I do shall he do also; and greater works than these shall he do; because I go unto my Father" (John 14:12). In the meantime, Jesus gives us increments of His power as we die to self and allow Him to abide in us in ever increasing measure.

I believe the demon-possessed man who lived amongst the tombs (commonly called the "Gadarene demoniac") was satanically ritually abused. The demons in him were so powerful he could break chains and fetters and no man could restrain him. Demons this powerful only come into a person through satanic rituals. No one picks up these kinds of demons through sinful living. Demons of this magnitude are specifically called up from hell and commanded to enter a person. The abusers don't want to be indwelt with these demons, so they have them put into their chosen special child where they can access these powers periodically. Of course, this child grows up and becomes an adult who lives in extreme torment from the abuse and the demons.

The fact that this man was tormented is obvious because the Scripture tells us he was crying and cutting himself with stones (Mark 5:5). It is quite common for people who were satanically ritually abused to cut themselves. It helps them cope with their inner emotional pain and gain some feeling of control over their own life.

The account of this man is recorded in Matthew, Mark and Luke. There are some differences between Matthew's account and that of Mark and Luke that have puzzled Bible students down through the ages. I believe when one views this man from the standpoint of SRA, these seeming discrepancies will be nonexistent.

The first seeming discrepancy is that Matthew says Jesus met this man in the "country of the Gergesenes," but in Mark and Luke it occurred in the "country of the Gadarenes." Some have suggested, in order preserve the integrity of the Scriptures, that there were two separate accounts where Jesus sent the demons out of the man into the swine. I think this is highly unlikely. Most commentators say this is the same account but that there was some confusion in the minds of the authors or the minds of those who copied the manuscripts as to where this actually happened. William Barkley explains it this way:

> The difficulty is that no one has ever really succeeded in identifying this place beyond doubt. Gerasa can hardly be right, for the only Gerasa of which we have any information was thirty-six miles inland, south-east of the lake, in Gilead; and it is certain that Jesus did not voyage thirty-six miles inland. Gadara is almost certainly right, because Gadara was a town six miles inland from the shores of the lake, and it would be very natural for the town burying-place and the town grazing-place to be some distance outside the town. Gergesa is very likely due to the conjecture of Origen, the great third century Alexandrian scholar. He knew that Gerasa was impossible; he doubted that Gadara was possible; and he actually knew of a village called

Gergesa which was on the eastern shores of the lake, and so he conjectured that Gergesa must be the place. The differences are simply due to the fact that those who copied the manuscripts did not know Palestine well enough to be sure where this incident actually happened. (Barclay 1975, 350)

Now I would like to offer my understanding for this difference of location. I believe the Scriptures are absolutely perfect and infallible in the original languages. There is no confusion in the mind of the Holy Spirit and the original writings were divinely inspired. Therefore, any seeming discrepancy was intentionally placed there by the Holy Spirit to teach us something if we will dig deeply beneath the surface of the Word to find it.

All proper names in the Bible have a meaning. Sometimes the Holy Spirit will reveal a deeper truth to us as we investigate the meaning of these proper names. This is exactly the case here in this passage. According to *An Interpreting Dictionary of Scripture Proper Names*, "Gergesenes" means, "those who come from pilgrimage or fight." "Gadarenes" means "a place surrounded or walled." These definitions will, I believe, support our contention that this man was satanically ritually abused. I believe the Holy Spirit placed both names here to expand our understanding of the spiritual message concerning SRA.

First we will examine the word, "pilgrimage," found in our definition of "Gergesenes." According to my 1828 *American Dictionary of the English Language* by Noah Webster, a pilgrimage is "a long journey, particularly a journey to some place deemed sacred and venerable, in order to pay devotion to the relics of some deceased saint." One meaning for "venerable" is "impressive on account of age or historic or religious associations."

Satanists like to hang around any place where there are the remains of deceased people—saint or no saint—so they frequently do rituals in cemeteries. Most people don't know this, but Satanists make a lot of pilgrimages. They like to do rituals in places they deem historically significant, especially places where there has been a lot of death. They believe they gain more power in these places because of the many spirits of the dead that they believe to be there and because of the powerful demons that hang around those places.

One of their favorite places for rituals in the twentieth century has been the historic concentration camps of Germany where millions perished during the Second World War. I know this because I have ministered to several SRA persons who had memories of being subjected to horrific rituals in these camps. Satanists like to do rituals in battlegrounds where large numbers of soldiers died and also in places of historic significance. If they can do a ritual at a national monument, for example, they believe they can gain power over a nation. Rituals have been done behind the famous Hollywood sign on the mountain near Los Angeles because, to the satanic mind, this is a way to increase the powers of the movie industry over the minds of the populace.

The second part of our Gergesenes' definition is "fight." This poor abused man had to fight for his life in order to survive these rituals and he did so by "surrounding himself with walls"—the definition for "Gadarenes." Satanic ritual abuse is so terrifying and painful that its victims learn to erect walls in their mind to seal themselves off from the memory of their abuse. They dissociate by saying, "That never happened to me," and then erect a wall of amnesia to shield themselves from the memory.

Speaking of memories—the Greek word for "tombs" where this man is said to have dwelled in verse two of this passage is *mnemeion*, derived from *mneme* meaning "remembrance" or "memory." Satanically ritually abused persons have much of their identity "entombed" in their memories. In order to survive their abuse, there had to be a split in the conscious process in which a group of mental activities broke away from the main stream of consciousness and functioned as a separate unit, as if belonging to another person. Because of this process, parts of themselves are locked away behind walls along with their memories causing them to feel less than whole persons. It is not uncommon for memories of several years of childhood to be totally lost from one's conscious memory because of the walls of "amnesia" erected in order to survive the abuse.

There is evidence from Scripture to indicate this man had multiple personalities. In Mark and Luke's accounts of him running to Jesus, there is only one man. In Matthew's account it reads, "And when he was come to the other side into the country of the Gergesenes, there met him two possessed with devils, coming out of the tombs, exceeding fierce, so that no man might pass by that way."

Is there some discrepancy here? It is obviously the same story, but in Matthew there are two and in Mark and Luke, only one. Notice carefully that in Matthew it says, "there met him two possessed..." but the word "men" is not there (KJ). It does not say two "men." It only says, "two." The answer to this seeming discrepancy is that there was indeed only one man but he had two personalities! (Some translations have added the word "men" here but it is not found in the original Greek.)

I believe the revelations being brought forth here concerning the Gadarene demoniac were divinely hidden—purposely written in such a way they could only be revealed by the Holy Spirit in the end times. It is the present day church that will be dealing with the phenomenon of satanic ritual abuse. The Holy Spirit would not have recorded the words "multiple personalities" for people down through the ages who would have had no knowledge of such a modern term. Therefore, it was carefully recorded that there were "two" but the word "men" was obviously left out. In this way it could be revealed in God's time for those who needed this information and could understand it.

Another interesting thing about this demon-possessed man is that he knew who Jesus was. The account in Mark tells us that when he saw Jesus "he ran and worshipped him." How did he know who Jesus was when even His own disciples did not yet recognize that He was God? Some have said this is because the demons knew who He was and because the demons knew, the man knew. I don't agree with this because I don't believe anyone worships Jesus due to the testimony of a demon. I believe He worshipped Jesus because He, himself, knew who Jesus was.

When little children are in the agony of satanic ritual abuse, they cry out to God for help, and He comes and helps them through their abuse. As a result of the rituals, their soul and spirit have experienced enough separation that they are open to the realm of spirit. This enables them to see, hear and feel the demons, which only increases their torment, but they can also see good spirits such as Jesus or heavenly angels. Satanically ritually abused persons, who have cried to Jesus for help, have seen Him and experienced Him in ways the rest of us have not. This man knew who Jesus was because when he cried to God for help during the rituals, Jesus appeared to him and helped him through. Over the years of SRA ministry, I have heard many testimonies from child alters about how Jesus was with them and helped them through their ordeal of suffering.

This ancient story also sheds light on the question, Can a Christian have a demon? Many Christians believe it is possible to be a Christian and still have an indwelling demon, but there are also many in the church who believe a Christian cannot have a demon. This question needs to be examined

more thoroughly if we are going to be able to help the satanically ritually abused who, when they were little children, had
demons purposely called into them by their abusers.

Many who were satanically ritually abused are desperate
for help but have nowhere to turn. Professional counseling
is costly and beyond the financial means of many; plus, few
professionals deal with casting out demons. Many satanically
ritually abused survivors are frustrated in their attempts to
find help from the church due to the church's narrow doctrine
of demonology.

If the Bible stated clearly whether or not a Christian could
have a demon, there would be no controversy; however, this
is not the case. Our belief on whether or not a Christian can
have a demon is based on how we interpret the Scriptures.
Perhaps the Holy Spirit intended it this way so our fellowship
with one another would be based on our love for Jesus rather
than our doctrine.

As we examine this controversial question, let us begin with
something I think we can all agree upon. In order to worship
Jesus, one must be a Christian. The Greek word for worship
is *proskuneo*, which means "to kiss (like a dog licking his master's hand);" "to prostrate oneself in homage," "do reverence
to," "adore," "worship." Clearly, no unbeliever adores Jesus,
reverences Him or bows in homage before Him. We must have
the Holy Spirit within to worship God in this way. Salvation
begins with a mental decision to believe in Christ and repent
of our sins. Only after salvation are we able to worship God.

The Gadarene demoniac was a man possessed by a legion
of demons (a legion, according to the dictionary would have
been between 3000 and 6000, or a vast multitude) who was
still able to bow down and worship Jesus. In spite of the demon possession, He knew Jesus and worshipped him. He had
to be, in modern terms, a believer or a Christian. Yes, he had
demons in him, but He was also a believer, which is exactly

169

the state of many persons today who were satanically ritually abused.

Persons who were satanically ritually abused have a light side and a dark side. They can love Jesus and experience His presence in a supernatural way—an experience of great exuberance—but in the same day, they may experience a cult alter coming forth and summoning demons which brings them down into despair. They experience great highs and lows, and are, therefore, often diagnosed as being "bipolar." If we look carefully at the state of this man in Mark's account, we can discern the Holy Spirit showing us this.

The scripture says, "And always, night and day, he was in the mountains, and in the tombs, crying, and cutting himself with stones." In "night and day" we see the dark and the light side of an SRA person. A mountain is a high place. A tomb is a grave or a hole in the ground, i.e. a low place. These extreme highs and lows coupled with the dichotomy of having a light and dark side, cause people to feel out of control and they may cut themselves in hopes of gaining some measure of control over their emotions and their troubled, confusing lives.

The response of the townspeople to Jesus is interesting. After Jesus cast the legion of demons out of the man and into the swine, the townspeople heard about what was happening and came to see for themselves. Mark tells us, "And they came to Jesus, and saw him that was possessed with the Devil, and had the legion, sitting, and clothed, and in his right mind: and they were afraid...And they began to pray him to depart out of their coasts."

This tells us volumes about the character of these people. One would think they would have been overjoyed to see this poor miserable man finally set free from his torment. There had to be no doubt in anyone's mind that Jesus was filled with the power of God and that He had performed a miracle. If this were so, why would they be afraid of Him? Some have said it was because they lost their swine. I think it was more than that.

There had to be, amongst those people, those who abused the man in their rituals and others who were under their control. They were afraid, not because of the swine, but because they knew they had come face to face with God, and Satanists regard God as their enemy. They didn't want to be exposed before Him or have to contend with the obvious truth that the power of God is far greater than the power of the Devil.

After this great miracle, the man who had been healed wanted to go with Jesus. Of course he wanted to be with Jesus! Who would want to go back to those people who had abused him and left him alone out there in the tombs? But Jesus' answer was, No. However, the Lord gave him some instructions. He said, "Go home to thy friends, and tell them how great things the Lord hath done for thee, and hath had compassion on thee" (Mark 5:19).

At first glance it would appear that Jesus was sending the man back to be with the people who had abused him. However, this was not the case. The man understood what Jesus meant and his response was, "...he departed, and began to publish in Decapolis how great things Jesus had done for him: and all men did marvel." He departed! He did not stay where he had been; he went out to Decapolis, the ten cities of the district of Syria, and testified of the great miracle Jesus had done for him.

When Jesus said, "Go home to thy friends," He did not mean what appears to us on the surface. Something has been lost in the translation. The Greek word for "friends" used here is *sos*. *Sos* is not the usual New Testament Greek word for "friends." The word "friend" or "friends" is in the New Testament 35 times and *philos* is almost always used. This passage is the only place in the New Testament where sos is used to mean "friend." *Sos* really means "thine," or "thine own," with "friend" only being implied. So Jesus was really saying, Go home to thine own. Who were "thine own" to this man? Other believers! He was now part of the family of God and other Christians were his friends.

There were many believers in Decapolis, as seen in Matthew where we read, "And there followed him great multitudes of people from Galilee, and from Decapolis, and from Jerusalem, and from Judaea, and from beyond Jordan" (Mat. 4:25). This man had a new family, the family of God, and he departed to those ten cities where he had many new friends and a whole new life awaiting him.

It is often needful for SRA persons to forsake their family of origin and find a new family because very often their abuse came from their own parents, siblings, aunts and uncles, etc. This is one reason why it is important for the church to understand SRA and embrace those who are recovering from its effects. We need to become their family. Holidays can be especially difficult for them because, not only do they no longer have an extended family with which to celebrate, but also, after having memories, they realize they were abused on holidays. Any holiday is a satanic ritual time—especially Christmas and Easter.

Some Christians have refused to believe in the existence of SRA because they say it is not in the Bible. However, it is seen in the Old Testament where parents made their children "pass through the fire" to the god Molech. Even the Israelites were known to do this because they did not heed the warnings of God to not intermarry with the nations around them. Because of intermarriage, they began worshiping pagan gods and even got involved in child sacrifice. This practice did not pass away with the coming of Jesus, and the story of the Gadarene demoniac gives us a view of Jesus healing one of its survivors. This should bring hope to all who have been so abused because we see here that Jesus understands and is able to heal anyone who has been satanically ritually abused.

Getting Started in Deliverance

Those who have never cast out a demon may feel fearful about attempting to do so. It can seem more difficult when demons are not manifesting because we may feel embarrassed about talking to something that may not be there, or we may fear that if something is there, we won't be able to handle it. When we approach this with prayer, knowing God has called us to help these people, then we have nothing to fear because God is in control.

My first attempt at deliverance occurred with a friend who was starving to death with anorexia. She said she hadn't eaten in about three weeks; she was taking laxatives and exercising strenuously. I tried to get her to go for professional help, but she refused. The two of us felt that she had a demon of anorexia and she wanted me to cast it out. I attempted to convince her to go to a certain pastor I knew who dealt with such things, but she was determined I was the one to do it. So, one evening, with much fear and trepidation, I told the demon of anorexia to get out of her in Jesus' name. I kept talking to it and in a few minutes she began coughing and out it came. She immediately wanted to eat.

I got some food out of the refrigerator, and she proceeded to eat for the first time in three weeks. I was elated. I had cured anorexia through deliverance--or so I thought. It wasn't that easy. The demon of anorexia came back into her the next day. Then I found out she had a demon of bulimia. The next thing I discovered was that anorexia and bulimia had a host of other demons that worked with them to destroy her life. I could spend hours casting them out, and she would seem to be normal, but then they would all come back in. That is when I learned it is a waste of time to cast out demons without ministering for the reason they entered in the first place. Whenever we do deliverance, we must discover why the demon was allowed in and deal with that or it will simply return again bringing others with it. (See Matthew 12:43-45.)

Demons are in ritually abused people because they were placed there through rituals and programming. For these demons to be cast out and kept out, memories must be told, curses and vows broken, alters converted, darkness renounced and faulty thinking replaced with biblical truth. All this must be done one memory at a time. There may be hundreds of memories, so at times it seems there is no end to the demons. After a memory and time of deliverance it is important to lock up with prayer all the remaining demons and alters before the person leaves.

In SRA we are not only dealing with demons that came in through past rituals, but also with demons that are currently being sent against the person. When cultists realize one of their own is telling memories and receiving deliverance, they declare war and begin networking. Satanic cults from many states or even other countries may send specific demons at your survivor in an attempt to stop her progress. (They will also send demons against the spiritual director. As long as you are called into this ministry and not walking in rebellion, there is nothing to fear. God doesn't call us to this ministry until He knows we are properly prepared by having a close relationship with Him. His protection covers us and our families.) Demons are sent to activate programming placed inside many years ago that was purposed to either bring her back to the cult or destroy her in the event she began talking. There are many such programs, and it may take months or years to dismantle them all. In the meantime, we walk by faith and trust God for her safety.

Not only are demons sent to activate programming, but also demons of voodoo are sent to attack her physical body. There may be many instances where she will experience unexplained sickness or pain. When an SRA person experiences sudden severe physical pain or sickness, I start breaking the curse of voodoo over her. If it is voodoo, demons will surface which need to be cast out. This usually brings instant relief from the physical distress. The Lord will often give the person a vision to show her what was done to the voodoo doll.

Knowing the Enemy

It is important in SRA ministry to differentiate alters from demons. It can be upsetting to an alter to be told to shut up and get out. One of the major ways to identify demons is by their character. They are totally, completely wicked without any trace of mercy, compassion or decency. They are extremely arrogant, totally deceived, and seem to truly believe Satan actually has more power than God. Sometimes they'll try to bargain with me offering me fame, fortune or greater power if I'll stop the deliverance. I have to laugh when they offer to give me more power because I obviously have far more power than they since I cast them all out...sometimes even in groups! And, I might add, after hearing the ritual memories, a person who knows Jesus would have to be completely out of touch with reality to have anything to do with Satanism as it offers only indescribable pain, misery, darkness and total defeat. They sometimes growl and snarl at me trying to scare me. I get right up in their face and say, "It is written..." Then they sometimes whimper, "You're supposed to be scared. Why aren't you getting frightened?"

I feel to add a word of caution here should there be any doubt in anyone's mind: demons are not to be pitied or helped in any way. They are fallen angels (Jude 6, Rev. 12:7-9, Mt. 25:41). They are totally, completely, despicably wicked and deserve nothing but to burn in the lake of fire prepared for the Devil and his angels. Redemption is for mankind only...

not for any spirit. Don't talk to them any more than is necessary to get them out. Although deceived, they are extremely intelligent, knowledgeable, powerful liars and deceivers. Apart from Jesus Christ we are totally at their mercy. Spiritual helpers who try to minister for SRA/DID apart from Jesus Christ may spend hours in fruitless effort because they, unknowingly, may be trying to minister to a demon masquerading as an alter.

If I'm not sure what is manifesting, I'll ask the Lord to show me. At that point the demon will do something to give himself away. I'll see him in the individual's eyes (a look of hatred and evil) or the demon will start to say or do something which exposes who he is. Sometimes a demon will be talking as though he is the person and when I ask the Lord to show me who it is, he'll slip up and use a pronoun in the third person rather than the first. For example, the entity speaking means to say, "Oh, I know I'm in no danger. It's perfectly safe for me to go to the party," but he'll slip up and say, "Oh, I know I'm in no danger. It's perfectly safe for her...uh, I mean me...to go to the party". Then I know it is not safe and she needs to make other plans!...and, of course, I cast out the demon.

One of the advantages of SRA ministry for me has been seeing how totally evil the Devil and his demons are. I want to flee from any thought or attitude in me that could possibly have originated from the darkness. It is difficult to find words to describe how completely inhuman and devoid of anything decent they are. When listening to SRA memories, one sees how completely overtaken by demons the perpetrators are and that there is not one ounce of pity or goodness in them when they are dominated by demons. People who dabble in the occult or give any credence to the dark side don't know what they're getting into. I even heard on Paul Harvey one day that one of our armed forces now has a Satanist priest! If people realized what Satanists do, they might arise from their complacency and begin to stem the tide of evil sweeping over our nation. To acquiesce to evil is to invite the greatest suffering and devastation to our country imaginable. God help us!

We must never try to gain information from demons because they are all liars. If I learn anything from them, it is in knowing the opposite of what they say is truth. Once when a survivor was living with us for a time of intensive ministry, I was preparing to leave the house. Suddenly a demon surfaced in her and said, "Whatever you do, don't pray over this house and don't pray over her!" They are terrible braggarts and fall right into the Lord's plans. All He has to do is tell them not to do something and they will immediately do it unless He prevents it.

It is not necessary to ask their name. Contrary to what some people have believed, we don't have to know their name before casting them out. It is true that Jesus asked a name from the Gadarene demoniac in Mark and Luke, but in Matthew he didn't ask for a name. Jesus, with his ability as God to know all things, must have known their name anyway. Perhaps He asked it for our benefit so we would understand how great a number of demons can be in one person. (Their name was *Legion* and a Roman legion at that time was probably about 6000 men.)

Demons work together in groups. I learned this during my first experience with deliverance concerning the woman who suffered from anorexia (and bulimia). This was before I knew I didn't need to ask their names. Before getting into the specifics about how they work together I want to make something perfectly clear here...people who suffer from eating disorders are not necessarily demon possessed. I believe the core problem in anorexia is a lack of identity. Demons can influence a person without being in them. Deliverance will not cure anorexia. As an anorexic person begins learning her identity in Christ, the demons will leave. Persons suffering from SRA have severe identity problems. With so many alters, they don't know who they are; therefore, they are often subject to eating disorders.

As I ministered to this woman, I saw how the demons were working together to kill her. The spirits named Anorexia and Starvation gave her a feeling of fullness in her stomach. A demon named Gluttony forced her to binge uncontrollably while Bulimia compelled her to vomit. Guilt made her feel guilty and sinful for eating. Haughtiness told her not eating would make her superior to others. Perfection convinced her perfection could be attained only if she didn't eat. Vanity caused her to believe that the less she weighed, the prettier she would be, and then she would be accepted by others. Pride caused her to take pride in being able to say, No, to food...something others could not do. Two spirits, Fraud and Illusion, worked together to make her believe she was fat when she was actually unhealthily thin. Worthlessness told her she didn't deserve to eat. Confusion made her confused about what or when to eat. Disobedience said she didn't have to eat when others told her to. Secrecy insisted no one should be allowed to see her eat. Fear made her afraid to eat. Manipulation used the eating disorder to help her get her way and disrupt her family. The Numbness spirit enabled her to bear the pain of starvation. Lies, Deceit and Deception caused her to lie about her eating habits.

In addition to these spirits, there was a group I've seen in many people that I call the "Death Group" consisting of Death, Destruction, Self-Destruction, Murder, Suicide, Ruin and Doom. In anorexia these spirits drove her to exercise vigorously (she walked several miles a day) and purge with laxatives. Besides these spirits, Insomnia kept her from getting adequate rest. Of course, these spirits are not limited to anorexia but one can easily see how they work together to destroy a person's life.

My approach to deliverance is totally different today. When I sense it is time to cast out demons, I just tell them to go. If a name pops into my mind I assume it is the Holy Spirit's prompting and I speak the name; however, knowing their names is usually not necessary. Telling a demon to manifest or asking it to speak its name through the survivor only prolongs their manifestation which is more taxing for the person. It is important in SRA that we not "go digging" for demons. They will definitely be there, but if we take the initiative rather than follow God's leading, we might trigger destructive programming, set off booby traps or bring up a demon we are not prepared to handle. Deliverance should be done in conjunction with memories, programming and breaking of vows and curses. If I'm not sure it's time to deal with a demon, I'll ask the Lord if He wants to deal with it. If He does, it will manifest.

Weapons of Warfare

God has given us many weapons to use in deliverance ministry. Here is a list of some I have found to be highly effective.

1. Quoting Scriptures - The Word of God is our sword of the Spirit and is very powerful for casting out demons. We need to follow Jesus' example when he was tempted by the Devil in the wilderness and said, "It is written..." The more of God's Word we have committed to memory, the more effectively we can wield this weapon. It is good if we can quote a Scripture that is the opposite of the character displayed by the demon. For example, quote, "...the joy of the Lord is my strength," when casting out Depression. We may not be that equipped with Scriptures so it is encouraging to know demons hate ALL Scriptures. If all we can

think of at the moment is John 3:16 then say, "It is written...for God so loved the world, etc." I usually quote whatever Scripture comes into my mind at the time believing the Lord is prompting me. Of course if we have never memorized Scripture, there won't be much in us for the Lord to bring forth. I recommend searching the Scriptures beforehand, writing them down and having them close at hand to read if necessary. Sometimes all I have to say is, "It is written..." and out they go.

One of my favorite Scriptures for deliverance is Luke 10:19: *Behold, I give unto you power to tread on serpents and scorpions, and over all the power of the enemy: and nothing shall by any means hurt you.* Another good one is Phil. 2:9-11: *Wherefore God also hath highly exalted him, and given him a name which is above every name: that at the name of Jesus every knee should bow, of things in heaven, and things in earth, and things under the earth; and that every tongue should confess that Jesus Christ is Lord, to the glory of God the Father.* Demons hate the name of Jesus or any reference to His blood. The Lord will guide you in finding Scriptures for effective warfare.

2. Praise Music - If you know beforehand you will be doing deliverance, have a boom box and a CD of praise music ready to play in the background as deliverance is proceeding. This makes the demons very uncomfortable and I'm sure weakens them. If I don't have this available, I sometimes sing praises to the Lord as the demon manifests, and it makes him leave. II Chronicles 20:21,22 says concerning King Jehoshaphat, *And when he had consulted with the people, he appointed singers unto the LORD, and that*

should praise the beauty of holiness, as they went out before the army, and to say, Praise the LORD; for his mercy endureth for ever. And when they began to sing and to praise, the LORD set ambushments against the children of Ammon, Moab, and mount Seir, which were come against Judah; and they were smitten. The weapon of praise used by the Israelites is just as effective today as we battle our enemies, the Devil and his demons.

3. Speaking in Tongues - Different kinds of tongues is listed as one of the gifts of the Spirit in 1 Cor. 12:10. *To another the working of miracles; to another prophecy; to another discerning of spirits; to another divers kinds of tongues; to another the interpretation of tongues:* This is highly effective in dislodging demons. I have heard several different-sounding languages come forth from my lips as I've used this gift against the demons. They understand what I'm saying even though I don't. They'll become indignant and say something like, "You have no right to say that to me!" or "Don't say that! Stop it! Stop it!" and out they go. Sometimes demons manifest speaking a foreign language... sometimes it is German and other times I don't recognize it, but I speak back with the language the Holy Spirit gives me and I triumph every time.

4. Anointing Oil - Sometimes anointing a person's forehead with oil will help dislodge demons. You may say something like, "I anoint this person with the holy (demons hate that word) anointing oil for healing and deliverance in the name of Jesus Christ." I may anoint their hands for service too.

5. Holy Water - I don't want to make any theological statements here about holy water. I'm only suggesting tactics I know are effective. Water is a symbol of the cleansing power of the Word of God and demons

can't stand it. In difficult deliverances I have taken a glass of water and quickly prayed, "Lord, make it holy" and sprinkled it over a person's head and the demon has immediately left exclaiming he can't stand holy water. There is no use debating whether or not the water is actually holy. The demons think it is and for our purpose that is all that matters. I haven't had to use this in the past few years but there was a time when I found this very helpful.

6. Love - I've had demons manifest telling me I should hate the person and saying degrading things about her in their attempts to disgust me. I sometimes give the person a hug and exclaim that I love her and then the demon leaves.

7. Forgiveness - Sometimes a demon won't leave until the person forgives her offenders. Once she professes forgiveness the demon flees.

8. Breaking vows - Vows are enforced by demons. Once the vow is broken the demon should readily leave. Sometimes a demon has to be cast out before a person is able to break their vow. It is common then to cast out a demon before and after the renouncing of a vow.

9. Breaking curses - If a demon is there because of a curse, he won't leave until the curse is broken. Pray and ask God to reveal any curses.

10. I believe we can ask the Lord to use any punishment or torture described anywhere in Scriptures. For example in Psalm 12:3 we read, *The Lord shall cut off all flattering lips and the tongue that speaketh proud things.* There have been times when a demon wouldn't shut up so I prayed, "Lord, cut off his lips and his tongue," and the demon was instantly silenced.

11. Blowing in the Face - It sounds a little crude to blow in someone's face but the more we become like Jesus,

the more our breath becomes His breath. If demons are being stubborn about coming out and I blow in someone's face, the demons have a fit and exclaim things like, "Phewww! How awful! You smell like Him. You stink. I can't stand this. Stop it!" and they leave.

Demon Tricks

It will be helpful to be aware of some of the tricks used by demons to stop effective ministry or halt the progress. One of their favorite tactics is to try to remove the person from the room. If they can't get an alter to take her out, then they may try to remove her through astral projection. If a survivor is beginning to talk but suddenly stops and her eyes begin to roll back in her head, she may be attempting to astral project. At this point, forbid the demon to take her out, ask Jesus to block every escape route, and command the person be brought back. At this point, the demon of astral projection needs to be removed and then ministry can continue. Personally I don't believe a person's spirit can leave the body and travel around in physical space, but something happens spiritually in astral projection that makes it impossible to continue relating to the survivor.

A certain author of several exceptionally good books about deliverance has said it is not necessary to go after a person who leaves the room when a demon is manifesting. This may be true in some instances, but it is never true in SRA ministry. Because demons have been given control of a person's mind and body through rituals and the person is programmed to self-destruct, none of these persons should be allowed to walk out of the room while a demon is manifesting. It is often necessary to physically restrain them. I am a small woman and most of my abused friends have been bigger and stronger than I, but I ask Jesus to help me, and we are always able to get the person seated again. Sometimes I just let go of the person when I am not physically strong enough and I say, "Jesus, You take over and please put her in that chair." It is amazing to see the person struggling and walking backwards and sitting in her chair!

In the ritually abused, demons do terribly destructive things as they are manifesting. They put the person's hands around her neck and try to strangle her. Sometimes they hit her face with her fists or try to kill her by a hard blow to her trachea. They may try to swallow her tongue. Since I have begun writing this book, the demons have tried to destroy this ministry by attempting to make a certain survivor die in my presence. She has come into ministry sessions with open safety pins in her mouth or large paper clips twisted into terrible shapes for her to swallow. Demons manifesting in her have grabbed her earrings, her barrette or even her wedding band and stuffed them into her mouth for her to strangle on right in front of me. As she is starting to choke, I frantically ask Jesus to get it out of her mouth. He always does but it is inevitably frightening. She has had a knife or other sharp object hidden in her socks or tucked in the neck of her blouse under her hair. She has gone into my kitchen, grabbed a knife and held it to her throat. They have tried to make her put her fist through the window or jump off the balcony of our stairs. She has to be physically restrained. I am not strong enough to restrain her myself so I pray for the Lord's intervention and together we control her. Their plan is to stop this ministry by having her commit suicide here in my house. They know they can't hurt me. If they so much as threaten me, Jesus does something I can't see that terrifies them. He doesn't allow one second of threatening talk to come against me before punishing them so severely they wish they'd never said anything.

When I say they must be restrained, I also want to add that caution must be used. If great force is used when demons are manifesting, a person can be injured. In SRA ministry a spiritual helper often must work alone. If I waited for someone to help me every time I cast out a demon, we wouldn't get much accomplished. People just don't have that much time. I think I have found a good combination... Jesus and me. I'm not physically very strong, but He is. He gives me strength when I'm restraining a demon. Sometimes I'll ask Him to hold the left arm while I hold the right and He does! It is amazing.

Another trick of the demons is to fool the spiritual helper by mispronouncing certain words. For example, the person needs to renounce vows, renounce certain beliefs or renounce darkness. Instead of saying, "I renounce darkness," for example, the demon will have her say, "I announce darkness," so it is important to listen carefully.

There are demons in some people who claim to be human personalities. In the most severely abused it is not uncommon for a spirit to manifest claiming to be her father and instructing you to leave her alone. This can be a most astounding display of spiritual strangeness. The person takes on some of the physical attributes, mannerisms and voice inflections of the "person" said to be manifesting. The first time I encountered it, I was totally mystified. The person manifesting this spirit is often convinced this is different from a regular demon and it certainly acts differently than other demons. This had me baffled because I had never read anything about this, and no minister or counselor I knew had experienced it. To persons who have not heard SRA memories, it may seem obvious that this is just a demon, but those of us hearing one bizarre memory after another begin to wonder about many things. It is quite an adjustment to listen to these strange and hideous things and then live normally in the world as we have always known it. We begin to realize our world and the culture in which we live are somehow not what we had thought.

Another difficulty we encounter as we try to understand these bizarre things is that the Bible seems strangely silent about so much of this. I searched the Scriptures trying to understand what was happening here concerning the "human" spirits. I wondered about Elisha asking Elijah for a double portion of his spirit. Could one person actually impart some of his spirit to another person? The answer is, No. The spirit imparted from Elijah to Elisha was the Holy Spirit. After much study and prayer, I am now certain these are just demons. Even when I wasn't sure what they were, I cast them out but I would be left wondering.

Demons are able to appear as departed human beings. Persons involved in occult activities may believe that Elvis Presley, Marilyn Monroe or Queen Cleopatra visits them at night and gives them instructions. This is total deception. According to the truth of the Bible, once a person dies he either goes to heaven or to hell. Departed human spirits are not allowed to roam around on the earth and appear to people. Ritually abused persons often have the experience of spirits appearing to them as their father, their mother or deceased perpetrators. This usually happens at night, with the spirits shaming them for talking and threatening them. This wields great power over the abused person and makes ministry more difficult. The survivor experiencing this is sometimes afraid to tell her memories for fear of the reprisals she will receive at night from her "parents" or whomever.

Another trick of the demons is to attempt to build a wall of division between the spiritual director and the survivor. They may cause her to have dreams where the spiritual director abandons or hurts her. To the SRA person dreams are far more real than the dreams experienced by the rest of us. Years ago when I first started this ministry, the Lord allowed me to experience one of these dreams to know what it is like. I had difficulty coming out of the dream and once I was awake, I was confused as to whether it really happened or whether I dreamed it. If a survivor seems withdrawn or afraid of you, it could be because of one of these dreams.

There are demons that twist your words so that what you say and what the survivor hears are two entirely different things. When it seems impossible to communicate, one of these demons could be working. Ask the Lord if that is the case, and if it is, He'll push it up for you to cast out.

One should be led of the Lord before bringing together a group of persons who have been satanically ritually abused. Each of them will have demons and programs that are destructive to one another. For example, we had two women in one of our churches who were ritually abused. Whenever they were together, one of the women lost all her strength to the point she had to remain in bed. As we enquired of the Lord, He revealed the other woman had a demonic program that sucked all the energy out of this woman. He revealed the program and we dismantled it, but then there were other programs. Demons jump from SRA person to SRA person and do destructive things to them. Until they are deprogrammed and delivered, their coming together should be at the leading of the Lord with much prayer. In our church we know this is happening and we deal with it through prayer.

Demons can program an SRA person. For example, if the cult wanted a survivor to go to the cemetery on Saturday night and wait for a man in a black car to pick her up, they send a demon with these instructions. The Lord will push up the demon for you to cast out but then you may need to pray and ask the Lord to remove the programming. If the programming is not removed, even though the demon is gone, the person will feel she is supposed to do whatever the demon had instructed. When the Lord removes the programming, the person's eyelids may flutter or there may be some other evidence that it is being done. The person will know when it is gone.

SRA children are sometimes forbidden to have playmates and the normal relationships and experiences of childhood.

These children are purposely kept isolated both physically and through inner programming. They are told that demons are their playmates and friends. Demons come to them looking like humans and offering to "help" them. This help may be, for example, a female type demon who encourages a little girl to let the men rape her telling her it's good for her, etc. These demons often have human names. If an alter is talking about her friend, it could be another alter but it could be a demon.

Knowing When Demons Have Left

Demons will leave people in different ways. During rituals demons have entered through all the orifices of the body and even through the navel. During deliverance they can leave in the same way. Sometimes we, as spiritual helpers, don't see any signs that the demons have left. The person receiving ministry may say that she feels peace or feels that a heavy weight has lifted from her. She may feel the Lord's presence. When she feels this way, we can assume the demons have left.

Usually, though, with SRA there will be manifestations with their leaving. The most common manifestation will be coughing. The demons will be leaving through the mouth by means of coughing but at the same time may be leaving silently from other bodily openings. Demons may leave as a person gags, belches, yawns, screams or howls. If demons came in through electric shock, the person's body will go through the spasms of electric shock as the demon leaves.

When it seems that the demons are gone, ask the Lord if He wants to push up any more. If nothing comes, then lock up all the remaining demons and secure the alters with prayer.

CHAPTER TWELVE

PROGRAMMING

The purpose of programming is to gain control of a person's mind, will, emotions and body to bring them into complete subjection to Satan and the cult. Through programming they are able to bring a person to the point of such servitude that any command or suggestion will bring immediate compliance. If they tell their victim to jump off a bridge, she will jump off a bridge. She becomes no different than a robot...they push a button...she moves.

The programmers use extreme torture, terror, intimidation, deprivation, isolation and demonization to break a person to the extent she becomes their obedient slave. Through these methods the identity is split and the personality fragments (alters) are assigned names and duties that work against the person and keep her controlled and subservient. After programming, the Satanists don't need to be present to control the person...her personality fragments take over and continue the abuse from within. Through programming the person is trained to hate herself and work constantly to keep herself physically, emotionally and mentally weak and in pain.

The cult delights in releasing one of their victims into society and controlling her from a distance. All they need to do is activate a program and the person becomes their puppet. Alters and demons run programs...the cult signals them to begin operation. Programming usually begins in infancy and continues through adolescence and even into adulthood.

Some programs run constantly...others operate when triggered. Each alter can be activated by some ingrained code giving the cult total access at all times. A program may be activated by a demon sent in by the cult or by a certain signal such as a series of beeps, flashes of light, certain numbers, a particular phrase or sentence, a certain voice, hand gestures, a musical motif, a certain picture, a siren, etc. Some programs swing into action on a particular date. For example, some SRA persons have been programmed to die at their own hands when they reach a certain age.

The kinds of programming are myriad. Programs are used to deprive the person of sleep, to punish her for eating, to punish her for not eating, to punish her for laughing or enjoying anything (it is not uncommon for an SRA person to beat herself with her fists for laughing), to keep her overworked and exhausted, to call curses to herself, to take her out to rituals, to punish her for receiving any praise or reward, to isolate her from people by breaking off any budding friendships, to act insane, to punish her for praying, to make it impossible to read the Bible, to commit suicide, to call cult members and report information, etc. Here is an interesting one...to forbid her to ever have another bowel movement should she begin disclosing memories! The list is endless. It is important for a spiritual director to understand that many physical and emotional problems in the SRA person may be caused by programming.

The cultists interfere with every part of the person's existence, depriving her of every one of life's pleasures including eating and sleeping. In spite of this, God always reserves a place inside the person that the cult can't touch. There is something of the real person, deep in the heart, that God reserves for Himself and they can't spoil it no matter what they do. As despicably horrible as SRA is, God does put limits on it. They can only go so far. When a person begins meeting regularly with a spiritual friend who has been called by God to the SRA ministry, God will put many limits on the programming. If He didn't, no one would ever come out of it. The accounts of God's supernatural intervention in the lives of these persons is marvelous and uplifting. My faith in God for my own life has grown immensely as I've seen how he saves His dear abused ones from the cult's programming and control.

An SRA person can be controlled by anyone who knows the codes that trigger the programs. For example, she could be assigned to travel in several different countries and anyone in those countries who knows the codes could completely control her. I don't have any proof for what I am about to say, but I believe certain individuals own these people and others pay money to be given a couple of codes allowing them to use her for a limited time in a limited way.

As stated previously, some programs are triggered by certain codes, but other programs operate continuously. For example, some persons are programmed with a work ethic that won't allow them to rest. They are compelled to work until they drop. They can't work on something for a few hours and come back to it the next day. They must work until the project is finished if it requires staying up all night.

It has been my experience that people don't want to know about SRA memories because they are so horrible; however, I believe anyone feeling called to SRA ministry needs to know about the brutality behind programming in order to understand the magnitude of the force that drives a person. Therefore, I am including here an example of programming that drives a person to work until she drops. What I am about to describe is no worse than what is depicted in *Jurassic Park*, a typical movie frequently aired over television. The monsters there were dinosaurs...the monsters here are humans.

Programming for Work

As a child, she had been flown to Germany every summer for programming...as had other girls from other areas. The programming was done by professionals with unlimited resources and usually took place in some secluded mansion where no one could hear or see what was taking place. The programmers would work on a group of girls at the same time. They would purposely allow the girls to form relationships so that later the girl with the least potential could be sacrificed as a means of gaining control over the other girls. The horror of the sacrifice would, of course, be magnified because it was happening to a friend as opposed to some stranger. (This is a common cult tactic.)

This particular group of girls was forced into hard labor while being deprived of necessary food and water. One girl began to tire and slack off from her work. She was chosen to be the example for the others of what happens when one doesn't work. In front of all the girls, they began to systematically chop off this girl's fingers one at a time. They continued cutting off body parts until the girl finally died. The remaining girls were then raped twice and forced to make written vows signed in blood that they would always work hard and do whatever they were told.

This is only one of several programs related to hard work found in one individual. This woman could never rest. As long as she was awake she had to be working on several things at once. She could never sit and watch television. She had to be working at some project at the same time. It was difficult for her to go to bed if the project wasn't completed, no matter how unimportant the work was...it could have been working a puzzle...something of no consequence but it had to be completed.

People subjected to this kind of programming will try to work themselves to death...even severe chest pains and a numbed left arm is not enough to stop them. Imagine what this kind of person is like out in the job world. Put her into a work situation with a boss who is open to demonic suggestion, and you have a slave...a slave to demonic control. People who do not worship Satan but are self-centered and open to darkness, given a place of authority over others, will drive someone like this mercilessly. All a demon has to do is whisper in their ear to assign more work and this employee will never stop until the job is done, even staying after work or taking work home to be done for no pay.

At this point, I believe programming will best be understood by examples. What follows, then, are examples of different kinds of programming found in several different women.

Programming to Go to Rituals

A woman who had been meeting with me for about a year realized she was going out to rituals during the night but she never had any recollection of having left her apartment. She would know she had gone out because she would be exhausted the next morning as though she hadn't slept. Sometimes there were marks on her body or a vaginal discharge for which she had no explanation. She would find clothing and shoes in a different location than they had been the night before. Periodically she would find the door unlocked in the morning even though she was positive she had locked it before going to bed. We began seeking the Lord as to how this could be stopped.

As we were asking the Lord about this, an alter named Sally Ann said she wanted to draw something for us that might be helpful. She drew the following picture of a robot but said she didn't know what it meant.

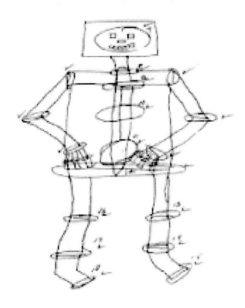

The next day as we were again asking the Lord about this, Catherine, an alter on level 14, surfaced and said she had the information we were seeking. Before she would give us the information, she wanted to pray for Jesus to be her Savior. (At this point in the ministry, many of the alters had seen other alters come to Jesus and receive His protection. To give out information was to invite retaliation by demons and cult alters.) After our prayer, Catherine drew the following diagram.

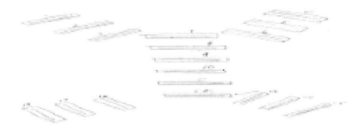

Here was a bird's eye view of what Sally Ann had drawn the day before. Catherine explained there was a demon in a box on each of this survivor's 18 levels. If we would cast out all the demons, she would no longer be taken out to rituals. This we proceeded to do. We began with the demon in one wrist, elbow and shoulder, and then did the same with the other arm. Next the head, down the spine and each leg. The most difficult demons to remove were numbers 6 and 13...favorite cult numbers that seem to have more power. By the time we were reaching the end, the demons departed quickly and easily almost as though they were frightened and knew they were defeated. Incidentally, the demons did manifest in each joint of the body. They were actually there in the places depicted in the diagrams.

A few days later I received a phone call from this lady early in the morning. That night (Saturday night...a favorite ritual night) she had been asleep in her apartment when she was awakened by knocking at her door. The knocking was in a rhythmic pattern that was repeated three times. She sat in her bed paralyzed with fear. A moment later a light was flashed through the window into her apartment, three times, in the same rhythmic pattern as the knocking. Shortly after this, she heard some sort of beeping, as with a small horn or electronic device with...you guessed it...the same rhythmic pattern repeated three times. She gathered enough courage to get out of bed and peep through the Venetian blind. She saw a woman holding some things in one hand and frantically waving with the other for the attending car to pick her up. She knew my friend was home but wasn't responding to the codes. There was no doubt she knew we'd found and dismantled the program.

Programming to Hit Self and Appear Crazy

I met an unredeemable cult alter named Nilda who hated Jane and wanted to hurt her. I physically restrained her hands because she had been repeatedly hitting Jane's face and throat with her fists. I asked Jesus to hold her feet, which He did. One of Jane's feet was injured and in an air cast. Nilda was

195

using her other foot to continually kick the injured one. Our conversation went like this:

Nilda: What's the matter with you?

Pat: I don't like seeing her hurt.

Nilda: Well, I love seeing her hurt.

Pat: You're just hurting yourself, you know.

Nilda: I don't care. I have plans and I will fulfill them.

Pat: What are your plans besides hurting her?

Nilda: I will destroy her.

Pat: But you'll be destroying yourself.

Nilda: I don't care. I have what I want and I have all I want. I have chosen this. I will destroy this body and I will destroy...

She had been tapping her fingers against her thumbs in a manner I recognized as calling demons up from the pit within. Sure enough, one big one after another began manifesting as I cast them out. They were powerful demons that clawed Jane internally, tried to swallow her tongue and convulsed her body as though she were being electrocuted. Suddenly the convulsing stopped as the last demon and Nilda were removed and the following words came forth from Jane in a monotone as though spoken by a robot...fast paced with no voice inflection and no emotion.

"I will stand here and you will hit me, and you will hit me, and you will hit me until I can stand no more, and I fall down.

If you are not here then I will hit me, and I will hit me, and I will hit me until I can take no more or I collapse. I must stay bruised. I must continually hit myself and keep myself under submission to my master. I must hit myself or someone must be there to hit me. I will keep my body in submission to my master. I will keep it in a state of pain. I must keep my body in a state of pain. I must keep myself bruised. For if I am bruised then others will not believe anything I might say that would reveal what is going on. I must keep myself bruised. I must keep myself bruised. I must keep myself bruised. If I ask people to hit me then they will know that I am crazy and no one will believe anything else except that I'm crazy. I'm weird. I must ask people to hit me, and if they will not then I must hit myself in front of them. Then they will know for sure that I am crazy. But I must keep myself bruised. I must hit myself to keep myself in submission to my master. My master wants me in pain at all times, and I have given him permission to keep me that way, and if there is nobody there to do it, I will do it myself. I vow this, and I declare this, and I agree to this. I will keep myself in pain. I will keep myself bruised. I will keep hitting myself, and hitting myself and hitting myself to keep my body in submission to my master."

Pat: What did they do to you to get this programming into you?

Jane: I was in a room and they would hit me and say, "You'd better get back up."

Pat: What did they hit you with?

Jane: Their open hand, fist...anything because it was either that or be raped. Of course, I got raped anyway, but I learned to stand my ground. I took the beating.

197

Pat: You weren't allowed to hit back?

Jane: Yeah, you could, but you had to hit yourself. That was your retaliation. They would make you so angry at them, but boy, you don't touch them. You were so angry you had to hit something so you started hitting yourself. You couldn't touch them. They would do this to you...punch you, punch you, punch you on one side and then they'd start on the other side and you wanted to swing back so bad but you knew you didn't dare touch them. Then you got so angry you had to hit something. It was just you and them, and you knew you didn't touch them. You knew from the past that you didn't touch them so...what would you do? You would hit yourself. Then they would talk to you and they'd say, You must keep your body in submission...you must keep your body bruised. And you finally signed papers...you signed papers in your own blood. They knew that if I asked people to hit me and they refused, I'd hit myself so they would know that I was crazy and wouldn't believe anything I said.

Pat: You need to break your vow, and Jesus will destroy that piece of paper you signed.
Jane: I break...uh oh, this demon is big. You don't want to touch this one.

Pat: Oh, yes I do!

I then cast out a tremendously strong demon. As soon as the demon was gone she began to cry that they burned her hands. She was screaming in pain. I could see the palms of her hands were beet red. She cried, "I wouldn't sign and they burned my hands. Oh, it hurts! It hurts!" I prayed and asked Jesus to heal her burned hands. The pain subsided quickly.

I asked what they used to burn her hands. She described it was like a hot iron but in the shape of a knob so it fit right into the palms of her hands.

She was then able to break the vows she made on those papers she signed. This was an extremely painful session, but she was freed from the compulsion to hit herself. Over the many months of our ministry and friendship, she had often begged me to hit her. There were countless times that I had restrained her hands to keep her from hitting her face with her fists. The day before we dealt with this program she had been hitting herself and arrived at my house the day of our meeting with a noticeable bruise on her chin and a large one on her arm.

Headaches

I met Nancy today, an alter who said she had been watching me for three years. According to Nancy, some of the other church people had been nice to Kay (the presenting person) in the beginning and then later hurt her, but she could see that I was different; therefore, she wanted to talk to me. She had the keys to the programs. She was free to roam up and down throughout all the levels in Kay's system. The demons who guarded the levels let her pass. She had many keys. It was her job to unlock the doors behind which lived alters in charge of the programs.

She opened one small room for me. We met Trixie. Trixie boasted that she had authority and had 49 people under her. Her job and the jobs of her people were to give Kay headaches. She had a doll's head that they used for voodoo. They poked pins into the head and tightened ropes and wire around it to give her headaches. One group of alters had pins, another group had wire, some had ropes, another group had clamps, and still others had hammers. These 49 people were spread out on the 13 levels. The ones on the lowest levels gave the most severe headaches.

I told her if she accepted Jesus she would have more authority like I do...she would have authority to tell demons where to go. She wanted me to prove I had power and offered me a challenge. She wanted to know if I could keep her from hitting Kay in the forehead. I assured her I could and that I would not use my hands. As I stood back with my arms at my side, she tried to hit Kay but was not able to do so. Jesus was holding her hands but she couldn't see him. She thought it was my power. This convinced her she needed to know Jesus like I do, but she was worried she would have to give up her important job. She prayed to receive Jesus and then obediently gave him the doll's head. Jesus gave her a songbook in return. Her new job was to lead the other 49 workers in praise to Him.

This dear lady left my office rejoicing over the fact she was headache free for the first time in many weeks.

Agitation

Lexi was in charge of a program to keep Thelma agitated at all times so she could not rest. Another part of this program was to cause her to take risks that could injure her. Lexi had 20 workers under her which all looked like little Leprechauns. Two of these workers were Dare-Dare and BeeBee. DareDare's job was to encourage Thelma to do dangerous things such as climb up the wrong side of the railing of the staircase, climb up the wood pile, or stand too close to traffic, etc. BeeBee had workers who were like busy bees to keep her thinking about all the things that needed to be done before she was allowed to rest such as dusting, vacuuming, paperwork, reading, etc. Nothing could be left half done. For example, if there were 10 pieces of candy in a box she had to eat them all even if it made her sick because nothing could be left undone. Because things can never be completely done, it kept her in a state of constant agitation so she could not rest mentally or physically.

Torment

Today I met Ethyl Daisy. She called herself E.D. because she hated her name. She was six years old and spoke with a lisp having recently lost her two front teeth. She lived on level 4 of the system in a little guardhouse. When the demons wanted to torment the survivor, they unlocked the door of the guardhouse so E.D. could perform her job. She would ascend the staircases to the top level and bring the presenting person down to level four. E.D. had keys to five rooms that were filled with demons. She would unlock one of the doors and thrust this person into the room to be tormented by the demons for a period of time. She had been programmed to influence the survivor to cut herself and hopefully wind up hospitalized should she begin talking to a Christian ministry helper.

E.D. said she really didn't like her job but she had no choice. I asked if there were demons guarding her and she affirmed this was true. I cast out the demons (there were four) and E.D. was then free to meet Jesus. Jesus took her to the playground to play with the other children. He destroyed the demons and their torture devices that had been in the five rooms. He redecorated the rooms with paint and wallpaper and then filled them with beautiful white doves.

Isolation

In actual life a new family moved into the apartment exactly beneath the one lived in by this survivor and her family. These new people started making strange noises every evening. One particular evening they were pounding downstairs in certain number sequences. For example, this survivor would hear bam, bam, bam eight times with a few seconds break, then bam, bam, bam five times with a few seconds break, then four and finally two. They would wait about two minutes and start the sequence all over again. About this time she went into a strange state of absolutely no emotions. It was as though she wasn't alive...her body just went through certain movements necessary for accomplishing her work. This was causing her to withdraw from relationships.

During our time of ministry I had no idea what to do to help her retrieve her emotions so I prayed in my prayer language and asked God to do whatever He needed to do. A few demons surfaced which I cast out and then I met Tommy, a hostile cult alter. He lived on level eight (interesting that the first group of pounding noises from the apartment below was eight.) He boasted about the power he had over her. I asked the Lord to remove Tommy's power source resulting in a few more demons coming out. At this point Tommy was very upset with me. I talked to him about Jesus, but he wasn't interested. He told me if I went any further I would cross over a line and I'd be sorry. I asked Jesus to do what needed to be done. Jesus came and removed the line that was designed to trigger a bomb should I cross over it. After removing the line and the bomb He talked to Tommy. He told Tommy that He loved him, but Tommy just couldn't believe it. Then Jesus laid His hands upon Tommy's and showed him the nail prints as He explained that He had died for Tommy. He asked Tommy to look in His eyes. At that point Tommy's resistance melted and he asked the Lord to be his Savior.

Then I learned that Tommy's job had been to go up through the levels to the top level, bring down the presenting person and lock her in an isolation room (which is what he had done when the pounding noises signaled him.) This had left her with no emotions. The cult's plan was that I would find out what happened and try to get her out of the isolation room myself, thereby setting off the bomb. Had the bomb detonated, she would have gone uncontrollably berserk to the point I would have had to call my husband to help me. He was to have insisted she be hospitalized and then force me to quit this ministry.

When a bomb is detonated in the inner world it thrusts powerful demons into every part of the person's body and they totally lose all control of their actions, words and thoughts. It often results in hospitalization and causes a tremendous setback in the healing process.

Jesus asked Tommy to unlock the room. Tommy would do so only if Jesus helped him, so with both of their hands on the key, they unlocked the room and let the presenting person out. Her emotions returned immediately. Jesus asked Tommy to go with Him to a safe place where other teenagers were (mostly girls) and asked him to help protect them. They walked to the safe place (a meadow filled with flowers) with Jesus' arm around Tommy in a loving, fatherly fashion.

Programming for an Assignment

She spent the night at my house. At exactly 12:45 A.M. her pager went off. She pushed the button revealing the numbers 719...that's all...just 719. Immediately a strong thought came into her mind to get a knife from the kitchen, come into my room and stab my husband and me. She cried out to God for help asking Him not to allow her to do what she knew she was programmed to do. He gave her the strength to withstand the programming, and eventually she was able to fall back to sleep after turning on the light and searching her room for possible intruders.

She told me about it the next morning. It was a frightening thing to know the cult had her pager number. We prayed. After dealing with three large demons, I met Bobby, an angry 19- year-old living on level 7. Now we understood the pager message of 719. It was to trigger an alter on level 7 who was aged 19. I learned from Bobby later that all the alters on level 7 were numbered according to age but other levels had different numbering systems. He was upset that he had failed in his assignment, and at that point tried to get a knife from my kitchen. With God's help, I was able to restrain him. Jesus came, calmed him and won his devotion. Bobby asked me if I trusted him. I answered affirmatively, and then he shook my hand. He had been given a new assignment by Jesus to show me where all the booby traps are on the first seven levels...not all at once but as ministry progresses.

Bobby said he was concerned about his unhappy four-year-old friend, Nini. He asked if I'd like to meet her. Of course I answered affirmatively, and soon I could see her crying and sucking her thumb. I started to touch her but she screamed and shrank away, so I stopped immediately. Bobby returned and said she had land mines strapped to her arms, legs and belly. If I touched them they would explode. She was often troubled because whenever I gave the survivor loving attention, the demons tortured Nini. Knowing that all alters have demons guarding them, I asked Jesus to push them to the surface for removal which He did. Then I asked Jesus to remove all the land mines which He did immediately. When I asked Jesus to minister to Nini, she shrank back in fear. He sent a white, woolly lamb to her. She giggled as she petted him and exclaimed about his little wet nose. She asked why his nose was wet but hers was dry...a typical four-year-old question! Then Nini asked me to touch her and hug her which I did. Jesus took her to the safe place with the other little children where she could play with the lambs.

Confusion

An alter named Scramble surfaced and bragged to me that it was his job to keep her confused by scrambling everything that came into her mind. He had a twin brother named Clog who kept her understanding clogged. The two of them worked together to keep her in a state of confusion. They lived on the first level of the pit. This survivor had thirteen upper levels and five levels in the pit for a total of 18 levels making Scramble and Clog's level 14. Each alter had four powerful demons empowering him to do his job. I dealt with Scramble's demons first. I always try to lead the alters to Jesus, but Scramble was too committed to darkness to want anything to do with Him, so Jesus removed him. Clog's four demons surfaced one at a time and were cast out. Clog also had to be removed.

The day after this ministry, this survivor reported to me that she was free from the extreme confusion and stress she normally encountered on her job.

Sadness and Depression

Inside of this 56-year-old woman was a shy four-year-old alter named Cathy. She hid her face behind one hand as she peeked at me from between her fingers and twirled her hair with the other hand. She spoke with a lisp. Her job consisted of continually reminding the person about terrible things said and done to her to keep her depressed. She lived alone in her room on level five except for the demon guards in each of the four corners who gave her the powers to depress this person.

I suggested she could be happy and have a much better job if she would be willing to make this person think good thoughts instead of sad ones. She didn't think she could do that. Jesus caused the demons to manifest one at a time so I could cast them out. Then I told Cathy about Jesus and asked her if she would like to meet him. She said, No, because she was afraid of men. I told her he was a kind and gentle shepherd and that seemed to allay some of her fears. Because of her fear, Jesus sent some little lambs first before approaching her. They nuzzled her about her face and neck, and she exclaimed delightedly over their cold little noses and the tinkling bells around their necks. After playing with the lambs for a few minutes, all her fear of Jesus had disappeared, and she wanted to go with him to the playground in the safe place. Jesus gave her a new job of taking care of the little lambs and helping this person think happy thoughts.

Programming for Sickness

An alter named Rebecca Lynn surfaced. She suffered from Tic Douloureux which caused her head to jerk towards her shoulder every few seconds. She said her job was to make Sally (the presenting person who did not have the tic) sick by putting curses on her. I led her in the sinner's prayer, and then Jesus came, touched her head, and the nervous tic ceased. She asked forgiveness for and broke the curses she had put on Sally.

Rebecca Lynn explained that she had been given a capsule by the cult that contained little beads. Her job was to release these beads into Sally's system making her sick. When I explained that the capsule contained satanic power and was used not only to make Sally sick but also to keep Rebecca Lynn a slave to the cult, she was willing to give the capsule to Jesus. (The cult frequently gives the alters certain objects that they are to guard at all costs. The alter frequently bases her identity on having this object and doesn't want to release it, not realizing it controls her.) Jesus opened the capsule and stomped on all the little beads as they fell causing them to disappear.

Rebecca Lynn's new job was to help Sally enjoy better health by encouraging her to eat lean meats, fruits and vegetables and bypass the sweets.

Programming through All Levels

It is helpful for the spiritual director to understand that some programs may be repeated on every level of the system and need to be dismantled in one session. A common program of this sort is the Insanity Program. It is important to the cult, once a survivor begins telling memories, to convince the spiritual director or persons close to her that she is mentally ill. If they can get her admitted to a psychiatric hospital, they can access her.

These insanity alters will surface and act totally, completely out of control. They'll drool, roll their eyes back in their head, make unintelligible sounds, bob their head around, wave their arms in the air, kick their feet and look totally out of their mind. This is all an act. They were trained to act like this or receive brutal punishment. Each one needs to be delivered of her demons and told the truth about Jesus. The Holy Spirit will intervene and give the supernatural help needed to deliver these alters. Insanity alters won't necessarily be on every level, but they commonly are.

CHAPTER THIRTEEN

THE ABUSE IDENTITY AND BACKWARDS THINKING

People having grown up in abusive homes think differently than those who were raised in loving, caring families. These different patterns of thinking are mainly centered in their concept of identity. Every human being is seeking answers to the questions, Who am I? and, Am I valuable? The answers to those questions will be answered early in life by our parents, family members and other significant people. If those around us in our early years are kind and loving towards us, we begin to believe we must be a good person...that we have worth and value as an individual. When we are mistreated and neglected, we decide we are bad persons having little significance, and we go through life with shame-based thinking. Persons with this kind of thinking face each day with a deep, gnawing feeling that somehow they just don't measure up...they're not good enough...everything about them is in some way flawed. They can't put their finger on any specific reason for this feeling...it's just "who they are." This brings hopelessness into a person's life causing many to despair of life itself. Instead of each day being a gift of life from God, each day is a trial...a test for survival...something one must somehow endure with no expectation of happiness or success.

When we face life with shame-based thinking, we expect to be mistreated, and we expect to fail. Because we have this mind set, others around us sense this and react to it thereby reinforcing our thinking of worthlessness and failure. It becomes a vicious cycle. The more we believe we are worthless and unconsciously project this image, the more others treat us accordingly. The more others give us negative responses, the more our negative thinking is reinforced. Within our soul, then, are deeply ingrained patterns of shame-based, failure thinking that are difficult to change. They are like deep gorges formed by years of torrential rainstorms that have eroded away the good soil and left us with valleys or deep gorges of painful identity thinking.

Abuse comes in many forms and degrees of intensity. This book has been about the very worst...satanic ritual abuse... but there are less severe forms of abuse that leave one with the same kinds of thinking...the gorges are just not as deep.

I have known people who were raised in Christian homes with parents who loved them but were unable to demonstrate that love for some reason. Some parents are just emotionally locked up, unable to give warm hugs and kind words of praise and encouragement. It is not uncommon for parents to withhold praise from a child for fear it would cause him/her to be prideful. Others, in their efforts to call their child to higher levels of performance, withhold praise thinking this will help their child excel.

Fred Green was raised in this kind of home. His parents loved him, took him to church every Sunday, provided a nice house in a good neighborhood and paid for his college education, but they never gave him the two things for which he desperately longed...demonstrable love and affirmation. Parents and children have two different concepts of love. Parents believe providing for their child's education, health and material needs demonstrates love...and it does...but children don't perceive this to be love. To children love is communicated by hugs, touching, listening to them and acknowledging them when they speak, looking in their eyes when communicating with them, playing games together, time alone with Mom or Dad where a child feels special, etc. Deep inside, children are asking the question, "Do you love me?" Parents need to constantly affirm, in ways children can understand, that they indeed are loved.

Fred's dad worked hard earning a good living for the family. When he came home from work in the evening, he sat in his favorite easy chair and read the newspaper. The only time he spoke to Fred was when Fred made a mistake or misbehaved. Then he reprimanded his son with a tone of voice that registered in Fred's mind as disgust, disdain and loathing.

Mr. Green had many talents. In addition to his profession as an accountant, he was an excellent mechanic and carpenter. He would spend weekends tinkering in the garage repairing or building something. Fred admired the things his father could do and longed to do them too, but his dad never trained him in any of these skills. If Fred tried to watch, he was told in an angry tone to get out of the way and go play.

Mrs. Green was a kind woman who sang in the church choir and did many kind deeds of charity in her community. She loved Fred, but Mr. Green had told her she was not to lavish hugs and kisses on her son. He wanted Fred to be a real man. There was to be none of this "sissy stuff" for his boy.

So Fred grew up longing to be hugged or to hear words of affirmation and praise from his parents. He tried so hard to earn their love and approval. Some children raised in this environment do many rebellious things to get their parents' attention because bad attention is better than no attention at all...but Fred was not like this. In fact, he tried very hard to earn his parents' love and approval. He was involved in cultural programs at school, but his dad never attended their performances. In college he played football hoping that would make his dad proud of him. Mr. Green attended one game and left early...that was it. He never came again.

Fran Blue was raised in a family that had worshiped the Devil for several generations. She had the unfortunate distinction of being the chosen child. Her ability to dissociate was phenomenal causing her to rise in the cult to the highest levels with the most sophisticated programming. She never wanted this; it was just something that happened to her because of the circumstances of her birth. All she knew in life was rejection and indescribable suffering.

Mr. Blue hated women and especially his daughter, so there was never one act of kindness or love shown to her. When he hugged her, he tried to crush her ribs and that, of course, was very confusing for Fran. She desperately longed for her father's love, but when he touched her, it was always painful. The only attention he gave his daughter was in brutal beatings, torture and rape. He actually enjoyed burning the private parts of her body with his cigarettes. That was his idea of fun. He constantly ridiculed her and deprived her of the normal experiences of childhood, even forbidding her to play. When Fran's brothers did something wrong, Fran always received their due punishment. (This is a common practice in cult families regarding their chosen child.)

The Blue family of six lived in a small, two-bedroom home in a tiny rural town. Most of the people in town were related in some way and most of them were active in the satanic cult. This made it impossible for Fran or her mother, who was also satanically ritually abused, to escape. The three sons shared one bedroom but Fran had to sleep on a cot in her parent's bedroom or on the living room couch. When her mother was hospitalized for months at a time, Fran had to sleep with her father actually taking her mother's place even as a small child. The abuse at the hands of her father was so severe if it were described here the average reader would be shocked and horrified. Her three brothers and seven uncles (also living in town) treated her with the same cruelty she received from her father and all of them wanted her powers. (See Chapter 5, The Purpose Behind SRA.)

Mrs. Blue loved Fran very much but had been brutally punished for showing her any affection or kindness. It seemed every time she demonstrated the slightest tenderness towards her daughter, Mr. Blue or one of the brothers saw it. This resulted in such cruel torture of Mrs. Blue and her daughter that she finally yielded to their demands. So by the time Fran was six years old, her mother had ceased demonstrating any motherly affection towards her. Although Mrs. Blue no longer showed any tenderness towards her daughter, she still loved her. At this point her love took a twisted turn. Because Mrs. Blue was also ritually abused, she knew the life of continual suffering her daughter faced. She decided the best way to love her daughter was to kill her, thereby freeing her from a life of misery. She would often say to Fran, "I wish you'd never been born. Why don't you just die?" In addition to the pain inflicted by her mother's words, Fran suffered actual attempts on her life by her mother. Mother tried to smother her with a pillow, drown her in the bathtub, stab her with a knife and twice left her lost and alone in the deep woods to die by exposure. However, God had a plan for Fran's life and saw to it every attempt was thwarted.

The contrast between Fred and Fran's upbringing is stark, but both felt abandoned emotionally causing them to have similar patterns of thinking associated with an abuse identity. The rejection they suffered as children was extremely painful, but it became a part of their identity. Both believed the lie, "This is who I am...a person whom others reject. This gives my life purpose and meaning." This belief was unconscious, of course, but it was a driving force in their lives. Every child forms an identity of some sort...even a negative identity is better than no identity at all. Whatever our identity may be, we are driven to reinforce it because the fear of nonbeing or no identity is unbearable.

Fred would unconsciously put himself in situations where others would reject him. Without meaning to, he would say or do things that would cause others to react negatively. He projected an attitude others perceived spiritually that broadcasted the message, You're going to reject me. So without understanding why they were doing so, they would reject him.

Fran also received rejection but to a greater extent and from almost everyone. She had SRA programming designed to keep her isolated (see Chapter 12, Programming). In addition to this, she was not able to do many of the things women do to make themselves attractive because, as a child, she was forbidden to have any nice clothing or wear makeup. This also became part of her identity. It is unfortunate, but people often judge us according to our outward appearance so Fran was often mistreated for this and other abuse related reasons.

Both Fred and Fran tried to protect themselves from the pain of rejection by hiding behind walls they unconsciously built in their souls. When Fred decided to hide behind his walls, he would sit at his computer in the basement hardly speaking to anyone. He didn't want to be with people. He would sit and play computer games for hours and dream of escaping to some rustic cabin in the woods where he could be away from people. After a few days of being quiet and withdrawn, he would come out of it and be outgoing and friendly and desire being with his friends again.

Fran was always hidden behind walls. No one really knew her and she didn't know herself. Her identity was split into many isolated fragments each locked away somewhere in the structure of her inner world, inaccessible even to Fran. She could put up a good front and act like other people, but her whole life was just that...an act. When rejection and pain became unbearable, she had thicker, higher walls behind which to hide. When she did this, she would sit alone, rocking back and forth with her eyes staring blankly at nothing, sometimes humming a little tune over and over. At these times absolutely no one could get through to her. Her body was there but she was totally inaccessible. Well, almost no one could get through to her. When she found a Christian friend who was committed to SRA/DID ministry, her friend would pray, "Dear Jesus, please bring Fran back to us." And Jesus would bring her back so her friend could help her.

Fran described the way she feels at these times. "I try not to let people touch me because that wall has to stay up. If someone touches me with kindness, the wall may begin to crumble so I have to make sure no one can touch me. I have to keep the wall strong so they can't see the real me. Nobody has ever seen the real me because I've never let her out. The real me is too scared and hurt to ever come out. She is locked away."

Fran instinctively knew the only thing that can bring down the walls is love. The way to bring people out from behind their walls is by loving them. This is one reason the body life of the church is so important. In today's mixed up world, many people have grown up in homes where love was not available. When families are so dysfunctional, the church needs to become the family for wounded people. In the safe environment of a loving church family, the walls can begin to come down, and people can safely rebuild their fractured lives.

Unfortunately many churches do not provide that loving atmosphere. Only if the church leadership purposes to make it so, is it possible. In our church we have many wounded people. When someone in our church continually hurts others, that person is confronted prayerfully by the leadership and asked to repent. If they refuse, they are disciplined in a biblical manner. Most people, when confronted this way, will leave if they refuse to repent. It is difficult when people leave a church, especially if every member's tithe is needed to cover the church budget or the pastor's job security is contingent upon growth in numbers. We have to, by faith, believe God will bring in new persons with gentler spirits to replace the ones who leave.

Both Fred and Fran suffered the pain of self-hatred. Fred would sometimes mumble under his breath that he was stupid and become depressed when he failed to meet his own demands for success. Fran was more overt in her expression of self-hatred. Sometimes she would beat her face with her fists until it was bruised while exclaiming, "I hate you, Fran! I hate you! Why won't you die?" Fran actually attempted suicide several times but Fred only thought about it and longed for death.

Both of them had unconsciously based their identity on the negative treatment they received as children. "This is who I am," they reasoned. "I will always be this way and there is no way out." Because of this mindset, they interpreted all of life according to this predetermined concept of self. Those close to them who loved them saw intelligence, creativity and many good qualities in them, but Fred and Fran were blind to it. The fact is, they were afraid to see themselves differently because as painful as their lives were, they at least knew who they were. They had become comfortable with their misery because it had always been that way for them. They didn't know if they could handle joy or success because then they wouldn't be themselves anymore and that was scary.

As strange as this kind of thinking seems, it is very common among abused people. This is why a woman will return again and again to an abusive, violent husband who beats her. She formed an identity as an abused child that this is her life...this is who she is. This identity must be reinforced or she faces the fear of the unknown or of being nobody. At least she understands a life of abuse. She wouldn't be comfortable being treated with kindness and respect.

Backwards Thinking

Satanists often purposely train their children to think in strange, backwards ways. The following is a transcription of a conversation I had with a child alter about backwards thinking:

Pat: Where, exactly, is this backwards room?

Susie: It is inside of me and there is a little area of my mind where they planted these wires that they can switch so things get mixed up for me. Even when I read, things get backwards. Sometimes I can read and read and read and never understand because it all gets jumbled because of these wires.

When you go to this room, they do things to you that make you very confused. They get you confused about right hand and left hand. They stand you in front of these mirrors and you can't figure out right hand, left hand, front or back...you're all mixed up. They turn the lights out and then they have these blinking lights and the mirrors, and you don't know where you've been or where you're going. You think, Have I been here? Is this a mirror? Is this a wall or a door? You go to grab for the door and you hit the mirror and it's very confusing. They have blinking lights... blinking lights that are almost hypnotic. A light flashes and you think you see this... and, boom, you hit something. You feel that and then you see this, and you go over here and you hit something else, and it's confusion and backwards and forwards and sideways, and you don't know where you're going.

But the clock ticks backwards...time, time, time, time... time goes backwards...time goes backwards...time goes backwards. You cannot go forwards. (At this point she was becoming hypnotic. She received ministry for this programming, and Jesus removed the backwards room. This child alter went to the safe place and the adult survivor continued to explain things to me.)

Survivor: It was total backwards programming. You got so used to doing things in this room that things that were right seemed wrong and things that were wrong seemed right. They did touch programming too. They would slap you and say, "This feels good." Then they would give you a soft touch and say, "This feels bad." Combing your hair felt bad but yanking your hair back harshly in tight braids felt good because it hurt and pain was good. Beauty was bad. A scratched face and blackened eyes were beautiful. Because of this, I'd rather have my face scratched and bruised than wear makeup. Good was bad and bad was good.

Examples of Backwards Thinking

In the simplistic language of the child alter in the backwards room, God's ways and thinking are forwards and any other thinking is backwards. The following are some examples of backwards thinking:

I have no right to have my own identity. I must take the identity of my abusers because they lord over me. I can't think for myself, so there is security in their power and control over me. If someone isn't controlling me, I don't know what to do. Someone good could not control me because my identity is, "I'm an abused person," so someone good could not reinforce my identity. Without that identity I am less than a nobody. It is better to be abused and be somebody than to be loved and be nobody.

To live in fear is a sense of knowing what is familiar and that feels safer than living in peace, which I know nothing about.

If you expect someone to hit you, at least when they do hit you, you won't be hurt as much because you were expecting it. (After four years of constant daily contact with this woman...she even lived in our home for over a year during which time she received constant, unconditional love... she would still sometimes draw back, raise her arm across her face and cry, "Don't hit me! Don't hit me!" This requires great patience on the part of the spiritual helper. Her abuse was so phenomenally severe that I've often wondered how she could have lived.)

Where do I belong? Do I belong with Mom and Dad? Do I belong with my uncles? Do I belong to these people they left me with that I don't know? When you don't know where you belong, you become insecure. Just when I started thinking I belonged to Mom and Dad, they would send me away. When I thought I belonged to my uncles, they sent me away. Is there any place I can go and be safe? If you belong nowhere you're not hurt when they take you anywhere because you didn't expect to be somewhere.

If I believe that I am no good, then I can't expect anything good to come from me, so then I won't fail. If I am already at the bottom of the barrel, then I can't fall any lower by failing.

If I don't sleep, I can't be surprised and no one can catch me off guard.

When I fall asleep, I am inviting sexual molestation and demons to come upon me.

A bad feeling I recognize helps me know I have identity. It is comfortable like putting on an old shirt.

I was programmed to be hurt. If something doesn't hurt me, I have to turn it around so it does hurt.

If anything good happens to me, something extremely bad will happen to negate it. If something good happens to me and nothing bad happens to negate it, I will die. Therefore, if something good happens I must make something bad happen so I won't die.

If anything good happens to me, I'll become selfish and self-centered.

It is selfish and sinful to pray for yourself.

If I let go of my past, I'll be a nobody.

I'm afraid if I release all my sins to Jesus, it will be too much for Him to bear.

To pray you have to empty yourself and chant the word, *Jesus.*

It is blasphemy to love Jesus and speak to Him personally.

I am so sinful, I contaminate the church. I shouldn't be in your house, because I will contaminate it.

Love scares me. I don't know how to handle it. My identity says I am an abused person, but your love is saying to me, No longer are you an abused person. This is taking away who I am, so I can't accept your love because then I would be nobody with no identity. Security is in knowing who you are even if who you are is negative. I'm abused. I'm a prostitute. I'm an alcoholic. If that is my identity, I am secure in that and I can't give it up.

Men equal pain. All men have authority over me and enforce it with pain. God made men to lord over women and control them.

I feel guilty that I lived when all those other babies and children died.

Anyone I love or get close to will die, and it will be my fault.

I don't deserve to have anything good. (I took this lady out to a restaurant for a nice meal. When we came back to my house, she went into the bathroom and threw up her dinner because she had enjoyed it. It was wrong for her to enjoy anything, and she couldn't bear the guilt.)

If I pretend my dad was perfect and good, then I can have a better relationship with God because your father is like God or God is like your father. I'm afraid to love God because He is like my father.

Feeling uncomfortable feels comfortable to me because it is all I know. To not feel uncomfortable would be scary.

As long as I live I must submit to my father's rules. His words are seemingly inscribed on my heart the way God said He would write His laws on our hearts. I can't get away from my father because he is inside me in the form of rules and memories. I am afraid to go against or denounce the rules because when I do, my father appears beside my bed at night and punishes me. (Her father had been dead for years. She remembered that all her life, even after her father died, if she ever asserted herself in any way or had anything good for herself, her father [a demon] would appear by her bed at night and punish her. She believed it truly was her father returning from the dead until I explained to her the truth--that spirits of departed human beings do not roam the earth and appear to the living. These are demons.)

I will destroy my parents if I go against their rules. I must always submit to their rules.

I'm so confused. One day Mom loves me, and the next she hates me. I don't know who I am. I hate my mother. If I hate her, then when she hurts me, it doesn't hurt as bad. If you love someone and they hurt you, it hurts so much you think you are going to die, so it's better if you don't love anyone. I hate me for hating my mother. The Bible says you'll go to hell if you hate, but I guess I'm going there anyway.

(There is terrible confusion when a parent is cruel. Instinctively we know it is wrong to hate our parents but some children are in a situation where they have no choice. They are too young and confused to do anything but respond instinctively to their abuse and thus hatred is deeply rooted in their heart. At the same time, they may be told they are to love and respect their parents. Some children handle this problem by creating another personality totally separate and opposite of themselves. This personality carries the emotions connected with the hatred setting the other self free to follow the demands to love their abuser. This confusion creates a powerfully strong self-destructive nature in the individual.)

I feel I am a nothing. I'm not a boy or a girl. Girls aren't acceptable to Mom and Dad, but I don't want to be a boy because boys hurt people--especially girls. My father said I'm like a capon.

(This woman had tremendous gender confusion. Her mother tired to convince her she was a boy to protect her. Her father told her she was a girl, and girls are objects to be used by men. Satan said she was a woman so she could be his bride. She didn't want to be Satan's bride, so she didn't want to be a woman. To admit she was a woman was to admit she belonged to Satan. Being a woman meant pain--like continually being raped or giving birth to babies that were sacrificed to the Devil.)

Satan keeps me in a mental state of confusion. I never know what to believe or what to accept. When someone comes and tries to straighten out my thinking, I get panicky. I don't know what it's like to think straight or focus. If I focused, then I would know what they were doing to me so it was better not to focus on anything. Confusion became one of my defense mechanisms, but at the same time they wanted to keep me in confusion so I wouldn't realize what was going on. If I understood what they were doing I might try to escape or change.

From Backwards to Forwards Thinking

The transformation necessary to change a negative identity to a positive identity in Jesus Christ requires a total change in thinking. This is extremely difficult and requires considerable love, time and sacrifice on the part of the spiritual director and the survivor's support persons. There is much more to abuse ministry than going through memories, deliverance or deprogramming. The false identity thinking needs to be identified, slowly dismantled, replaced with the truth of God's Word and reinforced with love and obedience. This is a long process.

Once again, a loving church is the perfect place for healing to develop. Often severely abused persons have no family members capable of giving the unconditional love and understanding necessary for these changes to take place.

Spiritual directors need to be aware of these different ways of thinking because the survivor is most likely unaware that anything is wrong with his/her thinking. They think most people have similar thoughts and that others see them the way they see themselves. An astute spiritual helper needs to recognize the basic beliefs lying beneath the surface of the survivor's conversation and behavior and bring them to their attention.

Once a negative thought pattern has been identified, there must be repentance for this thinking and a renouncing of it. Then the old thinking must be replaced with the truth of God's Word. In the ritually abused, there are often demons guarding these false beliefs that may have to be cast out. Sometimes there is a demon sentry guarding the belief who is removed first, followed by the strongman and his workers, and finally the root demon and his workers. When I do this, the workers are removed in a ball. (See Chapter 11, Dealing with Demons.)

Removing a false belief is like removing part of the foundation of someone's house. The Bible states that our foundation should be built of precious stones, (Isa. 54:11... *behold, I will lay thy stones with fair colours, and lay thy foundations with sapphires*) with Jesus Christ being the chief corner stone. He is the rock upon which we build. False beliefs are like ugly dirt clods in our foundation that easily crumble or wash away when the storms of life come causing the house to shift and shake. When this happens we often fill in the hole with another dirt clod rather than a precious gem of God's truth.

During ministry we want to slowly remove one dirt clod at a time and replace it with a beautiful gem mortised in place with love. Love is the mortar that holds the gems in place. For example, a ritually abused woman believes she is the scum of the earth...a piece of trash. During ministry we renounce that belief and replace it with Scriptures such as Eph. 2:10... *For we are his workmanship, created in Christ Jesus unto good works, which God hath before ordained that we should walk in them.* We need to understand that she isn't going to quickly believe this even though we've renounced the belief and cast out the demons. She has a deeply ingrained pattern of thinking about herself that has been with her for life and has been reinforced many times by the treatment of other people. It has become her identity. This won't be removed easily. She needs to memorize scriptures about who she is in Christ. She needs to obey God and incorporate the basic Christian disciplines of repentance, prayer and Bible study into her life. She needs to be around loving people who treat her as though she has worth and value. Gradually this old way of thinking will dissipate, and she'll be able to accept that she is indeed God's workmanship and He has a wonderful plan for her life.

All of us have believed lies about ourselves, life and God. We all have to go through this process of identifying false thinking and replacing it with truth. We all need a loving church environment and the disciplines of our faith to accomplish this. Severely abused persons need a little extra help, combined with compassion, understanding and lots of demonstrable love to overcome the deeply ingrained effects of their abuse.

CHAPTER FOURTEEN

POETRY BY ABUSED PERSONS

When I am in the depths of despair,
When the memories come from who knows where,
When the depths of my mind release the pain,
And I think that I will go insane,
Jesus is there.
When my body feels what the memories disclose
And the shock and pain increase and the anger grows,
Jesus is there.
When memories are so horrible, I try not to believe
But why the tears, anger and pain, that make me grieve?
Each childhood memory, each year, passes slowly before my
eyes.
Does anyone care? And I look and find
Jesus is there.
And He cries.
He cries with me for all the hurt.
He feels my pain and lack of self-worth.
He holds me like a little child.
He shields me as my fear runs wild.
He rocks me in a cradle so high
With guardian angels standing by,
Until I am able to cope once again,
He protects me from the world so grim,
My Jesus who is always there,

Who shoulders the pain I'm unable to bear.
He's always there to hold my hand,
And to pick me up when I can't stand,
My Jesus who is always there.

* * * * * * * *

Footsteps falling softly outside my door,
Footsteps walking across my floor.
Footsteps as faint as a baby's heartbeat,
Hands reaching under the bed sheet.
Now I lay me down to sleep,
I pray the Lord my soul to keep.
Don't scream or cry or make a peep.
Maybe this time he won't go too deep.
He likes to poke his fingers in there,
Poor, poor, child with skin so fair.
How nasty she's treated, I'm glad it's not me.
I'm glad I'm out here where I can be free!

* * * * * * * *

My name is Linda and I am not free,
My mind is in bondage and I am not me.
I feel lost and in deep despair,
To the point where I no longer care.

Lost from the present, lost from the past,
Feeling so lost, how long can I last?
There are days which seem so bad,
Dark and depressing, making me sad.

I began to switch before I was born,
On that cold November morn.

By the time I was three,
There were several people living in me.

When my father would make me feel bad,
Mimi would come and handle my dad.
She would take all the pain,
That surely would have driven me insane.

My family destroyed my body and mind,
Destroyed my will and I could not find
Any part of me that was truly real,
I had split so often I could no longer feel.

Mimi, Periwinkle, and Betsy too,
So many names it's like living in a zoo.
No matter whatever is the name,
The face is always still the same.

Who am I? Really soon I will know,
God will deliver me and heal my soul.
Then truly my mind will be free,
And I will be Linda, I will be me.

* * * * * * * *

There's a war going on inside my soul,
Demons and alters, trapdoors and holes.
Hurt, broken, lonely children...which ones are foe?
Which are friend? Memories flow
Through the poetry and then the flashbacks come
And won't let me be.
Horror after horror too disgusting to tell,
Abuse born in the very pits of hell.

No wonder people do not believe,
The pictures that are painted make your stomach heave!

* * * * * * * * *

Children born into darkness and fearful of the night,
But Jesus heard our cries and kept us through our plight.
What happened to the love that should have been shown?
Where did we hide all the horrors until we were grown?
In boxes, many boxes...that's where we hid them all!
And then we built the walls...sturdy walls
So they wouldn't fall down.
But all through our lives, behind the smiles were the frowns.
Eyes that could seem to twinkle in front of the veil,
That hid all the pain--it was a system which did not fail,
Until Jesus said, "It's time to let the memories go.
We'll bring them back a little at a time,
Because you need to know.
You need to remember so your healing can take place,
But I'll be there holding your hand
And covering you with My grace.
I'll not give you more than your shattered heart can stand,
And I will heal you as I hold you in My hand.
Just keep your eyes on Me and soon you will be able to see
Through eyes no longer filled with pain.
Just look to Me, Child, you have your wholeness to gain."

* * * * * * * * *

A childhood lost forever...innocence violated.
Nobody read me fairytales...I had to read them to myself.
There should have been butterflies to catch,
Piggyback rides to take, days at the park.
Do small children know what affirmation means?

Yes, they do!
It's hugs and snuggles and kisses on skinned-up knees
And good night stories...but where were they?

* * * * * * * * *

Darkness creeps unbidden into the depths of my soul.
A cold and damp feeling permeates and takes its toll,
An emptiness that's deep and wide,
As though something within me has died.
I feel a sense of loss, of something I can't touch or see,
And it travels the length and breadth
Of the boundaries inside of me.
What is it? What is it that I now search for?
The loss of innocence? Or my childhood?
If only I could reclaim it, I would.
But it's gone forever, taken away to the depths of hell.
And yet I know there's still more of the story to tell.

* * * * * * * * *

The clutch of death around my heart,
Its claws would love to tear it apart.
It stripped me of everything I should have had,
And slowly tried to drive me mad.
Wild clutching beasts from hell...
They were not human, I could tell.
If they were human, there'd have been love instead of hate.
If they were human, the child within
Would have had a different fate.
Swirling dark waters, pulling me down...
Don't want to fight anymore, please let me drown!

* * * * * * * *

Pierce my eye, pierce my heart!
Trample my body, tear my soul apart!
Lines of demons waiting their turn,
To pillage my body, to rape and burn.
Hideous faces, terror in the night,
Light a candle...burns so bright.
Victim after victim I see,
Oh, dear God, will I ever be free?

* * * * * * * *

Shadows dance across the floor.
She doesn't live here any more.
Don't know where she went to stay,
Someone said she drowned in the bay!
Has anyone seen her? I wonder where she went.
Next day they found her dolly all twisted and bent.
Does anyone know her whereabouts?
Will they ever find her? I have my doubts.
Something sinister, something dark,
carried her off into that park
Where children always disappear,
Causing parents to groan with fear.
Shadows dancing across the floor.
She doesn't live here anymore.

* * * * * * * *

Weird, twisted shadows in the night
Dance by the evil firelight.
Their breathing is raspy; their eyes look like death
And you can feel the fire of hell in their breath.
They will grab you and chop you and rip you apart

And then cut out your heart.
They love tender babies and children so small,
They devour as over them they crawl.
Whither thou goest, my little one?
Stay away from that park...
Turn around fast and run!

* * * * * * * * *

Oh, dear Jesus, please bring me back!
Please get me back on Your holy track!
Please wash me clean of all that is vile and obscene.
Please cleanse my body, soul and mind,
Break me free from the memories that bind.
Cleanse me now and make me pure.
I've remembered enough, no more can I endure.
Don't let me go back...let me rest for awhile,
While I renew myself. I can't go another mile.
The pain is getting much too strong to bear.
Please hide me under your wing
And don't let me go back there.

* * * * * * * * *

Running madly through the park
Try to escape that face in the dark.
Its eyes look hollow with fire inside.
It has no nose and it glows besides,
A hideous deathly green
I can't describe how mean.
Drip, drip, don't look back!
There's blood dripping in its tracks,
Hellish desire on its evil face.

I think I'm going to die in this place!
I want to scream, I want to shout,
But nothing will escape...nothing will come out.
Silent screams for someone to save me,
And God sends yet another one to take my place
And set me free.
He knew I could never stand all the pain.
He knew I'd die or else go completely insane.

* * * * * * * * *

Into a world filled only with evil,
Held captive in that hellish steeple,
Where things crawl and slither through the dark...
Don't let the children go near that park!
Their teeth are sharp and they rip at your soul and flesh.
They drink your blood and slobber on your face.
Their tongues lick at your body so small
And then they begin to crawl
Into every opening of your flesh they can find.
And then they try to take over your heart and mind.

But God in His mercy gives us a way to escape.
We break apart time after time
And each one hides in her special place.
God builds a maze with rooms in which to hide,
Thick walls and many, many floors to keep out the evil tide.
They think they've possessed you in body, soul and mind,
But the ones in the special places they cannot find.

* * * * * * * * *

Putt, putt, look in the jar,
A tiny boat...but it can't go far.
Round and round in circles so tight
It's such a sad, pathetic sight!

Mirror, mirror on the wall,
Who stole my favorite ball?

Someone punched it with a pin
Now it's losing air as its sides cave in.
Dolly, Dolly, with eyes so bright,
Who stole you away in the middle of the night?
They tore off your arms and your head
And now poor dolly is so very dead.

Little Boy Blue, with the little horn
Wishes he had never been born.
They poked out his eyes
And then ripped out his heart,
Then put him in that hole in that park
Where it's always dark.

Twinkle, twinkle in the sky,
How much higher can you fly?
High above your body so small
wishing all the time you could just fall
And then you'd be dead.
No more could they mess with your head.
No more could they inhabit your body and soul,
For their vile, inhuman, disgusting goals.
Will you ever escape this world so dark?
Will you ever escape away from that park?

* * * * * * * * *

It's time to let the darkness go,
It's time to let the East wind blow,
To carry away all you've held inside.
Let My hand brush away all the tears you have cried.
Remember that you're a child of Mine,
A branch upon My holy vine.
As you remember these things,
You must let them go
Or my healing waters will cease to flow.
Don't hold it inside,
Just lay it all in My hands.
Let My love surround you
While on the Rock you stand.

* * * * * * * * *

Witches dance by firelight,
Strange, unholy noises tear through the night.
What did she see...what was up there?
Was it really a baby? It's hard to tell
In the flickering fire's glare.
The fire can play tricks on your eyes.
She tries to look again as the little sounds die.
Maybe this time it was a dog or a cat...
Maybe, just maybe, it might have been that.
Hideous, growling noises from over there,
They told me don't go near...it's Satan's lair.
It's their feeding time.
I hear snarls and crunching of bones,
And there's another fresh patch of blood on the stone.

* * * * * * * *

THE STRANGER IN THE MIRROR

Who is this stranger that I see,
Looking out of the mirror, looking at me?
Just who can this stranger be,
She sure can't be a part of me.

I look in the mirror and I sigh,
Who am I looking at, O God, I cry?
Who am I looking for and who is she?
Who is the person looking back at me?
I turn to one side, then to the other,
Wondering just why should I bother.
Is this strange person the real me,
Or is this just a stranger that I see?

I put on my makeup; she does the same.
Then I punch myself and wince in pain.
The funny thing that I see,
Is that she is acting just like me.

At this time the tears begin to flow,
O God, who is the person that I don't know?
Lord, is this a stranger that I see,
Or is she really a true part of me?

* * * * * * * *

PERIWINKLE

My name is Periwinkle
But I'm not really blue.

I am a very happy child,
And I would like to play with you.

I come and go whenever needed,
Just like all the rest.
I love to make the others laugh,
But I love my Jesus the best.

Jesus is my very best friend,
He knows me by my name.
He comes to play with all the children,
And He knows my favorite game.
When Glenda becomes very sad,
Scared and closes down,
She often dreams of being free,
To skip and play around.

That is when I come up,
To let her play inside.
Her mind becomes the playground
Now she can swing and slide.

Why is it that I'm here now?
Why do I come and play?
The darkness no longer holds her down,
No longer am I held at bay.
Now I am free to come and go,
And make faces in the mirror.
I tease my mommy all the time,
And she really thinks I'm dear.

I am a special part of Glenda,
A part that will never die.
A personality of love and joy
So she won't have to cry.

A PHILOSOPHY OF SRA MINISTRY

It is my belief that ministry to the satanically ritually abused needs to be totally Spirit-led. Ministry should flow forth out of faith in Christ and our oneness with Him. Ministry to satanically ritually abused persons does not have to be difficult as long as we do it by faith trusting in Jesus to lead the way.

Probably most, if not all, Christian counselors who minister for SRA/DID would say they are led by the Spirit of God in ministry. However, since "Spirit-led" means different things to different people, I would like to clarify what I mean by the term "Spirit-led." The best way to do this would seem to be by illustration and example as follows.

When I am ministering to an abused person who has dissociated into several parts (MPD/DID), I ask the Lord Jesus to bring forth for ministry whatever parts of the person (alters) He chooses. He determines which alters I speak to, and He determines how many will present in any given ministry situation. This way I know I'm not breaking into the system in an area that is not ready for ministry where I could inflict damage. Neither am I overloading a deeply wounded person with more intervention than she is prepared for at that time.

I like to think of an SRA/DID person's inner system of alters as being like a house of cards with booby traps dispersed throughout. If I decide where to minister, I might pull a card out from the foundation of the system and cause some structural damage. Jesus alone knows where the core persons and the original person are located, and He alone knows when it is best for them to be found by me. Therefore, I do not purposefully go looking for them by asking questions of presenting alters.

As each alter presents to me after having been brought forth by Jesus, my entire ministry is directed to her specifically. She is the most important person in the system at that time, and she has needs that must be met. After ministering to her, Jesus places her in a safe place within the inner structure of the survivor's inner world. Then Jesus brings forth the next alter He has chosen for ministry at that specific time. This way I am not penetrating any area of the system that is not specifically targeted by Jesus because I am not making any of these decisions. The Lord is doing the work. This is what I mean by being Spirit-led.

Prayer is an important part of SRA/DID ministry. When I minister there are three persons present—the survivor, the Lord Jesus and me. His presence is very evident in supernatural ways that astound me.

When Jesus is allowed to be completely in charge of the abuse ministry, demons only manifest at His discretion. I do not go looking for demons or try to make them manifest. Jesus brings them forth in His timing. In this way I know I can handle whatever comes because Jesus would not bring forth a demon for me to deal with if I were not fully equipped to do so. This gives me a sense of confidence and assurance in deliverance ministry. Sometimes I just ask the question, "Jesus, do you want us to deal with this alter's demons now?" That's all I have to say, and it either manifests or He indicates we have more to do before we deal with it. Sometimes I don't even say that—Jesus just pushes it up at the right time without my having said anything.

This approach is very comforting for the wounded SRA/ DID person who is already suffering from painful memories, horrifying demonic manifestations, health problems and all the other difficulties faced by dissociative persons seeking help. The only demon battles they are forced to endure are those Jesus deems necessary.

Our power over the demons comes from oneness with Jesus not the specific words we say. The more we have allowed the deep working of the cross in our lives, the greater the power of Christ will be in us. Through this oneness we know when to pray and how to pray. He leads us in renunciations when they are applicable. This way our prayers are Spirit-led, and ministry can proceed quickly and efficaciously.

Integrations are also completely at the Lord's discretion. I do not decide when to integrate or who integrates into whom. The Lord in His perfect timing does all this sovereignly.

My approach to SRA ministry reminds me of something I learned growing up as a flutist. I was constantly preparing for music performances. My preparation consisted of every kind of scale, scales in thirds and fourths, all manner of arpeggios and volumes of etudes. I devoured etudes. I did not spend nearly as much time on my concert pieces as I did on the basics. As a result of thorough preparation of the basics, my concert pieces came together under my fingers with ease.

I see SRA ministry as being like the concert piece. The time I spend in prayer, study of the Word and meditation with Jesus are like the scales and etudes. As a result of much time spent in His presence, the ministry flows with ease at His direction.

Those of us who minister for satanic ritual abuse or those who are sensing a call to this kind of ministry need to be very careful that the supernatural manifestations that are unavoidably part of SRA ministry do not distract us from our pursuit of Jesus. We can easily be led into enemy traps of studying occult literature, using human reasoning to find explanations for the phenomena we see, or allowing the time we could spend with the Lord to be wasted on learning about things that are best left to the Lord. A deep study of God's Word, using a concordance, can uncover many secrets about the spirit world that can be learned in Jesus' presence without contamination from the darkness of the occult world.

God's loving concern for us is expressed in this passage from II Corinthians:

"I am jealous over you with godly jealousy: for I have espoused you to one husband, that I may present you as a chaste virgin to Christ. But I fear, lest by any means, as the serpent beguiled Eve through his subtlety, so your minds should be corrupted from the simplicity that is in Christ" (II Cor. 11:2, 3).

WORKS CITED

Barclay, William. 1975. *The gospel of Matthew*. Vol. 1. Louisville: Westminster John Knox Press.

Barna, George. 2003. *Think like Jesus*. Nashville: Integrity.

Crabb, Larry. 1999. *The safest place on earth*. Nashville: Word Publishing.

de Fenelon, Francois. 1992. *The seeking heart*. Jacksonville, FL: SeedSowers

de Tocqueville, Alexis. 1835. *Democracy in America*. Quoted in Doug Newman. "Because America is Free," available from www.freerepublic.com/focus/f-news/526019/posts (accessed 17 January 2004).

Guyon, Jeane. 1975. *Experiencing the depth of Jesus Christ*. Sargent, GA: SeedSowers.

Jukes, Andrew. 1891. *The new man and the eternal life*. London: Longmans, Green, and Co.

Kluger, Jeffrey, "Young and Bipolar," *Time*, 19 August 2002, 39.

Murray, Andrew. (n.d.) *Humility*. Old Tappan, NJ: Fleming H. Revell.

Nee, Watchman. 1965. *Release of the Spirit*. Cloverdale, IN: Sure Foundation.

Sandford, John and Paula. 1982. *The transformation of the inner man*. Tulsa: Victory House, Inc.

Sparks, T. A. (n.d.) *What is man*. Quoted in Watchman Nee. *Release of the Spirit*, 8. Cloverdale, IN: Sure Foundation, 1965.

Thomas, Ian. 1961. *The saving life of Christ*. Grand Rapids: Zondervan.

AUTHOR INFORMATION

Patricia Baird Clark prayed for many years, "God use me in a ministry that is initiated by You, empowered by You, and brings You glory." In 1985 God answered that prayer by bringing a succession of troubled women to her door commencing a ministry that brings healing for the most severely abused...those ritually abused in satanic cults. In more recent years the ministry is also to men as her husband, Dr. F. Stoner Clark, has joined her in this ministry. For many years as co-pastor alongside her husband, she has devoted herself to intensive Bible study and unlimited hours of SRA ministry... even having abused women live in her home during concentrated periods of ministry. As a result she has unlocked many secrets of satanic ritual abuse and DID which she reveals in her book, *Restoring Survivors of Satanic Ritual Abuse: Equipping and Releasing God's People for Spirit-Empowered Ministry.*

With no formal psychological training she has been able to bring people with diagnoses such as Schizophrenia, Paranoia, Bipolar Disorder and Borderline Personality into complete remission through Jesus Christ. One of these women had been hospitalized in psychiatric hospitals seven times, heavily medicated and given electric shock treatments. No one had ascertained she was severely abused or had dissociative identity disorder.

Patricia has a B.A. degree from the University of Indianapolis and is the author of two other books: *Sanctification in Reverse: a biblical exposé of satanic ritual abuse alongside end time truth* and *The Four Living Creatures: entering God's kingdom in the age of terror.* The Clarks have two daughters and six grandchildren. Before entering the ministry, Patricia enjoyed playing in symphony orchestras and chamber music groups as a professional flutist. She and her husband are amateur photographers who mat and frame their own wildlife and nature pictures. The cover of this book is one of her photos.

Patricia may be contacted through her website at www. hispresenceonline.org.

CPSIA information can be obtained at www.ICGtesting.com
Printed in the USA
BVOW030002081111

275507BV00001B/6/P